PRAISE FOR MIND CALM:

'Sandy has the ability to explain how you can get true calm in mind and body with ease and without struggle. No matter how fast paced your world is, no matter how chaotic or conflicted your life is, Mind Calm will give you all the insights and tools to get what you want, when you want it. If you want peace, love and happiness, Mind Calm is the book for you – read it and digest it all. You will not regret it.'
JOSEPH CLOUGH, BESTSELLING AUTHOR OF BE YOUR POTENTIAL

'Mind Calm is a simple yet brilliant tool for being at peace with our innermost irritant thoughts. Sandy expertly shares usable techniques for a life-enhancing meditation practice that results in less stress. This is a book I will recommend over and over to my clients.'
BECKY WALSH, RADIO PRESENTER, COMEDIAN AND AUTHOR OF YOU DO KNOW

'I'm always inspired by Sandy's teachings. In this practical book, he shows that you don't need years of meditation practice to enjoy inner calm in your life.'
PHIL PARKER, ORIGINATOR OF THE LIGHTNING PROCESS AND AUTHOR OF GET THE LIFE YOU LOVE, NOW

'Mind Calm reminds us that happiness is an inside job. Filled to the brim with guidance that is straightforward yet profound, Sandy Newbigging has carved the path to finally finding peace with our minds. This book is a must read for anyone ready to welcome more simplicity, serenity and success into their life.'
CHRISTY FERGUSSON, AUTHOR OF HOT, HEALTHY, HAPPY

'Sandy writes with such lucidity and calm. It would actually be quite difficult not to become calm while reading this book!'
DAVID R. HAMILTON PhD, AUTHOR OF HOW YOUR MIND CAN HEAL YOUR BODY

'I love this book. I can see myself using it time and time again to, as Sandy suggests, "surrender to what is", "go with the flow" and "simplify my life". Oh the joy of a mind that is calm.'
RICHARD FLOOK, AUTHOR OF WHY AM I SICK?

'Mind Calm is packed full of fantastic information that not only calms the mind, but elicits a potential that moves us towards "genius". The book allows the reader to fully realize that if we only listen to the mind, we quickly tire of its discourse. Whereas if we silence the mind we connect with Source. Hurrah for MIND CALM!'
STEWART PEARCE, AUTHOR OF THE ALCHEMY OF VOICE

CLIENT TESTIMONIALS:

'Mind Calm offers tools to experience the incredible peace, love and fulfilment that you've been looking for.'
S. POWERS, CANADA

'Mind Calm has brought more peace into my life and people have even commented that I'm laughing more (which I've noticed myself doing, too). Overall, Mind Calm has given me a greater sense of wellbeing.'
U. WALSHE, IRELAND

'Since learning Mind Calm, I can access my inner peace at any moment choose. I don't have to be sitting in my meditation practice to do it, but I can be calm at any moment when going about my everyday life.'
J. BRYANT, UK

'The best thing I've got from Mind Calm is the understanding that I can let my thoughts and emotions come and go, and get back to my calm conscious awareness. It is such a free experience. After years of trying to strive for 'peace of mind', I can actually live a very serene life by developing a better relationship with the mind I have – it's just fantastic.'
S. McLAUGHLIN, IRELAND

'Mind Calm has been the best gift I have received in my life – allowing me to move from having boring days at work, always waiting for the weekend, to be able to have fun and excitement about life – every day.'
M. TSACHEV, BULGARIA

'I love Mind Calm because I have found so much joy, peace and presence in my daily life, and it's just getting better and better.'
S. BUTTIMER, IRELAND

'Mind Calm has given me a real sense of serenity. I can catch myself when I'm getting caught up in my mind, which allows me to come back to the present moment. Overall, Mind Calm has given me a better experience of life and I don't know anyone that doesn't want that.'
J. GRAHAM, SCOTLAND

MIND CALM

MIND CALM

The Modern-Day Meditation Technique
that Gives You 'Peace with Mind'

SANDY C. NEWBIGGING

HAY HOUSE

Carlsbad, California • New York City • London • Sydney
Johannesburg • Vancouver • Hong Kong • New Delhi

First published and distributed in the United Kingdom by:
Hay House UK Ltd, Astley House, 33 Notting Hill Gate, London W11 3JQ
Tel: +44 (0)20 3675 2450; Fax: +44 (0)20 3675 2451
www.hayhouse.co.uk

Published and distributed in the United States of America by:
Hay House Inc., PO Box 5100, Carlsbad, CA 92018-5100
Tel: (1) 760 431 7695 or (800) 654 5126
Fax: (1) 760 431 6948 or (800) 650 5115
www.hayhouse.com

Published and distributed in Australia by:
Hay House Australia Ltd, 18/36 Ralph St, Alexandria NSW 2015
Tel: (61) 2 9669 4299; Fax: (61) 2 9669 4144
www.hayhouse.com.au

Published and distributed in the Republic of South Africa by:
Hay House SA (Pty) Ltd, PO Box 990, Witkoppen 2068
Tel/Fax: (27) 11 467 8904
www.hayhouse.co.za

Published and distributed in India by:
Hay House Publishers India, Muskaan Complex, Plot No.3, B-2,
Vasant Kunj, New Delhi 110 070
Tel: (91) 11 4176 1620; Fax: (91) 11 4176 1630
www.hayhouse.co.in

Distributed in Canada by:
Raincoast, 9050 Shaughnessy St, Vancouver BC V6P 6E5
Tel: (1) 604 323 7100; Fax: (1) 604 323 2600

A catalogue record for this book is available from the British Library.

ISBN: 978-1-78180-262-5

Printed and bound by CPI Group (UK) Ltd, Croydon, CR0 4YY

To all Teachers from all traditions who
have shared the universal message:

'Be Still and Know Who You Are.'

CONTENTS

FOREWORD

Have you seen the Monty Python comedy sketch '100-Metre Dash for People with No Sense of Direction'? Picture the scene: John Cleese, Michael Palin, Eric Idle and the rest of the runners are at the starting line. They are impatient and agitated as they wait for the starting gun to fire. Finally, the race begins, and everyone races off in different directions – meaning no one gets to the finishing line, no matter how fast they run. This sketch is a perfect metaphor for our mad-dash world, manic lifestyles and the chronic busyness that repeatedly takes us to our knees and makes us feel there must be a better way.

Where does this pressure come from to live so fast, to be so busy and so manic? Is it from society? Our upbringing? The media? Sandy Newbigging recognizes the external pressures, but he encourages us to look closer to home. In *Mind Calm*, he shows us how to liberate ourselves from the inner mind-made pressures that cause us to race for our lives. What Sandy helps us to do is to stop suffering from our own psychology. He helps us to be the thinker of our thoughts instead of the victim of our thoughts. He offers us liberation from fear, judgment and attachments.

In my work as a coach I see that *most people don't need more therapy, they just need more clarity.* Sandy sees this too. He takes us beyond the fix-it approach. He helps us cultivate a healthy relationship with our mind. That's his approach: *peace with mind.* Sandy coaches us on how to befriend our own mind, and he does it brilliantly. Step by step, he shows us how to stop suffering from psychology, so to speak, and to cultivate an awareness that makes an inner shift from *becoming happy to being happy.*

My encouragement to you is to read *Mind Calm* with an open mind. Read it slowly. Don't race to the end. What you are looking for is on every page, not just the last page. Enjoy the journey. Sandy has filled *Mind Calm* with lots of insights, epiphanies and exercises that are truly enlightening and helpful. Give yourself to the programme Sandy has created for you, and as he says, *'let the loving hand of the universe guide you.' Mind Calm* is an inspiration, and I recommend it wholeheartedly.

Robert Holden PhD
Author of *Shift Happens!* and *Loveability*

Preface

CHAOS BEFORE THE CALM

Turning points often come when you least expect them. Mine certainly did. Everything was going great. Business was booming. I was on television in 30 countries around the world. My courses and clinics were full. I was running residential retreats at stunning resorts. I had books out with mainstream publishers, was appearing in newspapers, magazines and on radio too. I had a great girlfriend, we were living in an upmarket part of Edinburgh, driving fancy cars and had more money than I thought possible. On paper, I was living what many would deem a successful life. Then one day I woke up to a really scary realization: despite everything going so well, on the inside it was a very different story.

Stressed to the hilt, I wasn't experiencing an iota of peace. I spent most of my days swinging between feelings of frustration and fear. Frustrated because I wasn't quite 'there' yet and when I did eventually get what I thought I wanted, I quickly moved into a state of fear about losing what I'd worked so hard to achieve. I could feel lonely in a room full of people, and nothing relieved the enduring itch that 'there must be more to life than this'. Physically, I found it hard to sleep with the mayhem going on in my mind. I struggled against persistent tiredness and was getting ill more often than I would care to admit, especially as I was working in the field of 'health detox' at the time. In a nutshell, I felt like a failure and fraud and a million miles from the peaceful happy self that I so yearned to be.

CONFUSED YET CURIOUS

It was around that time that a friend recommended I try meditation. I remember politely declining, saying that I couldn't meditate. To which they enquired, 'How do you know you can't meditate?' I was perplexed at first as to how to answer because, prior to my friend's enquiry, everyone else had always agreed with me that meditation was difficult. That day, after thinking about it for a few moments, I gave my main reason for why I couldn't meditate: 'I cannot stop my mind.'

Temporarily happy with my answer, I was immediately thrown back into confusion when my friend joyfully declared, 'Ah, well you don't have to stop your mind in order to enjoy peace when meditating.' To be honest, her response sounded ridiculous. Everything I'd read and heard about meditation up until then had all pointed to a 'still mind' being the main prerequisite to peace. However, she was suggesting the opposite. Could it be possible that I could have a busy mind and still be peaceful? Confused yet curious, I knew that all my attempts to stop my mind hadn't worked, so I agreed to learn to meditate.

MEDITATING FOR MONTHS WITH MONKS

Soon after learning to meditate, I began to notice that I was experiencing a surprising amount of serenity. So much so, I went on a 10-week meditation retreat to the Greek island of Patmos with the monks who taught me, and then spent a further 14 weeks in the mountains of Mexico, with month-long retreats since. During these times I had the opportunity to meditate all day and night, occasionally up to 18 hours a day, and received great guidance along the way. As you can imagine, diving into such intensive periods of meditation is transformational, bringing with it inner and outer changes both positive and profound.

After graduating as a meditation teacher, I immediately started sharing it with everyone who showed an interest. Having discovered that enjoying inner peace was easier than I thought, it became clear to me that I wanted everyone to experience the calm and contentment that meditation can bring.

WHATEVER WORKS FOR YOU

Even though meditation is certainly not religious, many of the techniques taught are ancient in origin, and so some of the recommendations and rituals might be perceived from the outside as being religious. Consequently, those disinterested in such offerings can find 'meditation' in general unappealing.

I'm a firm believer in 'different strokes for different folks'.

I'm not here to judge or tell you what you should believe or which spiritual path you should take – or if you should walk any spiritual path at all. The most important thing to me is that you don't miss out on the boundless benefits possible from meditation. I want you to experience the calm and clarity, connection and liberation that are everyone's birthright – when given the guidance and techniques that are right for them.

In my desire to share the benefits of meditation with as many people as possible, I became inspired to offer a form of meditation that anyone can use. With Mind Calm, I'm sharing an accessible way of meditating that draws on what I've learned from thousands of hours of meditation, which anyone can use to make the move from mental chaos to mind calm.

Having found calm and contentment in my life, I know that if it is possible for me then it can be for you, too. Mind Calm is a modern-day meditation technique that can help you to still your mind at will and be at peace with the mind you've got. You will discover that peace with mind equals peace with life – which is not only a very delightful way to be but also the secret to a truly successful life.

Sandy C. Newbigging
December 2013

ACKNOWLEDGEMENTS

'Be still' is the simple yet profound message shared by great sages, spiritual masters and enlightened teachers from countless traditions. The recommendation to 'be still' isn't about learning concepts or ideas about stillness, but an eternal invitation to experience it directly and discover the relationship between stillness and knowing the beauty and magnificence of who you are. To all of the sharers of this universal message, I honour and thank you deeply. Without your courage, clarity and commitment, I might not have discovered the delights of stillness in my life.

In relation to this book, I would like to thank the Hay House team who believed in me and this message, including Carolyn Thorne, Michelle Pilley, Jo Burgess, Amy Kiberd, Julie Oughton and, of course, Reid Tracy and Louise Hay. Big thanks also go to my excellent editor, Sandy Draper, for the improvements you made during the edit. And to Robert Holden for writing a fantastic foreword.

I wrote the first draft of this book during a seven-week trip around California with my girlfriend, Laura. I want to thank you, Laura, for being there when I wrote the first word, all the way through to when I sent the final manuscript to Hay House. You bring joy to my journey and I feel blessed every day. Special thanks go to Sasha Allenby for your friendship and allowing me so freely to share our Reawakening Protocol within this book. I would also like to thank my family for their unconditional love and unending encouragement, and my wonderful friends Bryce Redford, Calum Murray, Suzi Gibson, Sue Masters, Richard Abbot, Lee Johnson, Micci Gorrod, Andrew Pepper and Narain Ishaya for being a constant source of fun, love and inspiration in my life. I would also like to thank the family of Mind Calm Coaches from around the world for sharing this meditation with joy and clarity.

Finally, infinite gratitude goes to my spiritual teacher MKI for being my guide in this lifetime on the bright path of joy that is stillness.

Be Still.

Introduction

THE SILENT SOLUTION

How do you know you have a mind? You are aware of it, right? By that rationale, within you now exists a mind and something that is aware of your mind. This book is about becoming much more interested in, and attentive to, the conscious awareness that is aware of your mind, instead of going to any great lengths to fix, change, manage, manipulate or improve it. Mind Calm gives you a new relationship with your Self, which can be the determining factor in whether you experience what can be described as a hellish life, full of stress, struggle and suffering, or quite literally nirvana now.

Conscious awareness is still, silent, spacious, peace-filled presence; it is not otherworldly, but as real as you can get. Consciousness is the calm context of every thought, feeling, action and circumstance in your life – whether they appear to be positive or negative. Knowing and directly experiencing the conscious awareness that is present within you is the silent solution to any stressful situation that you may be facing and the secret to enjoying a truly successful life; free from fear, problems and limitations.

Full of potential, creativity, happiness, and grace, getting to know the conscious awareness residing within you offers the ultimate love affair — oneness with your Self.

Contrary to what you may have been taught to think and believe, you will discover that being at peace with life is the master key to engaging a truly success-filled existence. Rediscovering the inner reservoir of calm residing within your conscious awareness – always – transforms your relationship with your thoughts, emotions, body and life. No longer needing to work so hard to perfect your mind, emotions and external circumstances, you become at peace with who you are and how life is.

WHAT IF YOU ARE NOT WHAT YOU THINK?

One of the main reasons why so many people miss out on the exquisite experience of their conscious awareness is that they're having an identity crisis. Quite simply, they think they are someone or something they're not. They think they are the voice in their head and, as a result, rely on what it says too heavily for defining who they are and what they're capable of. They think they are what they are feeling emotionally. They think they are their body, having identified with it from an early age. Or they think they are their relationship status, job title, religious affiliation or the long list of other labels that they've found to help define who they are.

Wanting to 'know thy self' is part of being born human. It is normal to be on the search to find meaning from all of the potential sources listed above. Whether aware of it or not, there's a big chance that you, too, have been exploring the answer to life's big question: *Who am I?* Without guidance it is extremely easy to fall into the understandable assumption of thinking that you are the temporary and transient traits that so many others think they are, too:

- I must be the voice in my head because it sounds like me.

- I must be my emotions because I feel them inside me so intimately.

- I must be my body because it's been with me since I was born.

- I must be my job title because that's what I tell people I am when asked what I do.

- I must be my relationship status because my marriage certificate says so.

- I must be my religion because it is what I believe in so strongly.

The list goes on and on. But none of these things are ultimately you. Yes, they contribute to your personality and what you tend to do with your day, but that does not make them you.

Why? They are all temporary, come and go and change. Therefore attempting to find your Self in these transient labels is a bit like trying to stay still in the ocean without an anchor. It's not going to work and you'll find yourself drifting. Moving from one mental construct to another can be very confusing – not to mention highly stressful – if you attempt to define who you are from the things in your life that constantly change and are, to a large extent, outside your immediate control.

What if you are not who or what you think?
Are you willing to explore a new way of
perceiving and experiencing your Self?

I AM AWARE

When I refer to your 'real Self', I'm speaking about the permanent aspect to you. The dimension of you that does not come and go or change, and is not temporary. The aspect of you that is present – always.

During literally thousands of hours of meditation, I've explored this big question and come to conclude: I am simply the Self that is aware. Everything else is a mind-made creation or life circumstance that comes and goes. But that which is aware does not. So who are you? You are the conscious awareness that is aware of the voice in your head and all the other thoughts and emotions happening daily. The awareness that is aware of your body and all the physical sensations and conditions that occur. The awareness that's aware of all of your relationships, bank balance, the jobs you do, the houses you inhabit and the hobbies that you happen to love.

Awareness is the one facet of you that has been
with you your entire life and you've never
for one iota of a moment existed without.

Even if you've been unaware of it, your conscious awareness has been fully present the entire time. Consciousness is what still exists when you are not having thoughts or emotions. It is forever with you despite the people in your life moving on, your job titles changing, your body growing older, your home addresses moving and so on; it is the contextual landscape in which everything else in your life occurs.

MIND-MADE PROBLEMS

Believe it or not, problems are made up by the mind. This potentially shocking possibility is so because without the mind's interference through judging things as negative, bad, wrong or worse, life happens without anything being experienced as problematic. Yes, tricky, unexpected and perhaps unpleasant things may occur, but the mind needs to judge things negatively for them to be deemed a problem.

> *Buddha was once quoted to have said:*
> *'No mind, no problem.'*
> *And it is so true.*

Owing to the way the mind operates, if you spend your days thinking then you can end up stuck in a never-ending cycle of problem-solving and finding new things needing to be fixed. The unfortunate knock-on effect of being unaware of consciousness and caught up in the myriad of mind-made problems is having a body under copious amounts of stress, living on an emotional roller coaster of ups and downs, and ultimately a sense of never feeling truly satisfied or successful in business and life.

STILL SILENT CONSCIOUSNESS

Beyond the mind exists a still silent consciousness that holds within it the solution to any mind-made problem. By solution I don't mean an answer that comes from clever or positive thinking but a way out of the box of the thinking mind altogether.

Until I knew still silent awareness and the pristine peace, limitless love, joy and unbounded abundance that it contains, I never felt totally satisfied with the life that I'd worked so hard to build. Always feeling like 'there must be more to life than this', I chased goal after goal in the hope that the next tick on the list would bring me true satisfaction. I thought I wasn't happy yet due to my life not being how I thought it needed to be. I simply hadn't ever considered that my discontentment could be coming from the fact that I was living lost in my pendulum-like mind – swinging from judgement to judgement – and as a result of this unseen habit, inadvertently missing a huge aspect of my life and my Self.

> *None of my achievements could ever relieve the eternal itch that something was missing. I was simply looking for fulfilment in places that it couldn't be found.*

No amount of money can buy you the inner peace and connection, fulfilment and happiness that you naturally and immediately experience when engaging present moment awareness. All these wonderful things are built into the fabric of your conscious awareness. Available to you now, no matter how positive or perfected you make your thoughts, emotions, body and life. Does this sound too good to be true? Keep with me and stay open-minded!

Having been involved in this field of work for a decade, I've worked with a whole spectrum of individuals; some of them almost broke, others multimillionaires. Irrespective of the size of their bank balances, however, everyone is equal when it comes to having the same abundant awareness living inside them. The richer folk haven't necessarily been any happier; they've just had different problems to deal with. It's become clear to me that true success is not measured by external means, but by how calm, contented and connected to your real Self you are on the inside.

During this journey to a new way of experiencing your mind, your Self, and life, I hope you will clearly see that the secret to success is stillness.

CONSCIOUS AWARENESS LIFE MEDITATION

Mind Calm is a simple, easy and fun modern-day meditation technique for being consciously aware in life. 'CALM' stands for 'Conscious Awareness Life Meditation', and it is a way to meditate that does exactly what the name suggests.

Through meditation with your eyes open and closed, you can become more consciously aware during daily life. This book will give you guidance on how to use Mind Calm along with the know-how you need to be able to practise it with ease and in the most effective ways.

A MEDITATION METHOD FOR 'PEACE WITH MIND'

'Peace with Mind' is not a typo. Far from it! The term is one I've been using for a while and has been my main inspiration for writing this book. With Mind Calm I would love to put 'peace WITH mind' on the map.

I've observed that peace of mind is perhaps one of the most confusing and demoralizing spiritual incentives on the planet, as it implies totally clearing your mind of thoughts for good. Yes, permanent peace of mind is possible. Not to mention marvellous – for the few who manage to attain it in this lifetime. However, that's my point. To reach such a state of mind–body harmony, where thoughts are permanently stilled, can take many hours of meditation, very precise guidance on how to let go of the mind's subtle attachments and, in some cases, a good dose of divine intervention.

In today's world most people have incredibly busy lives. They balance career pressures with family and financial responsibilities, which all take up the bulk of their time and attention. Even if they wanted to disappear off to a monastery somewhere, to meditate for months in a quest to find permanent peace of mind, for most people this simply is not an option. As a result, achieving this state can seem like a pipe dream. So far from the realms of possibility, it can unfortunately make meditation seem to be an ill-affordable luxury in an already full schedule.

So it is for those people, who make up the bulk of the current population, with whom I'm keen to share Mind Calm, along with the very appealing and achievable possibility of 'peace with mind'. I have also found this approach to be highly beneficial for people who have already worked on 'waking up', as it provides a bridge that anyone can walk to be more consciously aware and find calm on the inside.

Mind Calm offers a solution that is not just for making your mind still, but also for making peace with your mind when it inevitably starts moving again.

Stopping your mind from having thoughts is possible. You are going to experience this is true when you play with the Mind Calm Games shared later in this book. Never having another thought again – i.e. permanent peace of mind – however, is an entirely different ball game. Especially when you take into account how much the average person's mind is stimulated and overworked. Also, if you happen to like your mind, it can be an unappealing suggestion that you should never think again. So Mind Calm is a solution that enables you to coexist peacefully with your mind. It is my hope that you are also willing to explore what exists beyond your mind, to find the aspect of your radiant real Self that deserves your attention too.

CALM WITHIN THE APPEARANCE OF CHAOS

Being consciously aware, you create space between you and your mind. Putting your attention on this space leads to an immediate inner calm. Not because you have stopped your thoughts necessarily, but due to experiencing the still silent presence of your own conscious awareness. With practice you can find that the calm continues, even if you start having negative thoughts or emotions. Or even if you are having challenging physical issues or unexpected difficulties arise in your external life circumstances.

How remarkable is that? You don't need to stop your negative thoughts or emotions in order to enjoy inner calm, neither are you destined to be negatively impacted by the unpredictable nature of your life circumstances. You can be free to enjoy calm irrespective.

This liberated way of living comes from healing your relationship with your mind, emotions, body and life. So once you learn how to get Mind Calm any time you want, by being consciously aware (see Chapter 4, page 43), the rest of the book is about making it a habit to be at peace with your thoughts, at peace with your emotions, at peace with your body and, eventually, at peace with your life in general.

Mind Calm offers a two-part path of peace and prosperity:

- Part I: Peace of mind (sometimes), and
- Part II: Peace with your mind (the rest of the time)

Until you are in harmony with life, you can gather as many riches as you like, but you won't necessarily be living a truly successful life. I want your calm, clarity or contentment never to fall victim to the movement of your mind. I want you to discover that when you are at peace with your mind you are at peace with your life. Ultimately I want you to know how, by stopping your mind whenever you want and also being unaffected by your mind when it inevitably moves, you can transform your relationship with life for the infinitely better.

THE STILL SILENT INFINITE I

Conscious awareness is inherently still and silent. A sign that you are aware is that you experience inner stillness and silence. It is my hope that reading this book is an eye opener for you. Not solely from a conceptual perspective, but that you experience what I refer to as the 'Infinite I'. Spoken about by countless spiritual teachers over millennia, the Infinite I (or 'infinite-eye', if that makes more sense to you) is the awareness that is observing life unfold and the consciousness that all of life exists within. You have front-row seats at this glorious adventure called your life. It is time to say 'bring it on' and welcome whatever happens with wide-open arms.

To get started, let's explore why you have such a busy mind, so that you can make the move from so much mental activity to mind calm.

The lotus leaf is often used to symbolize the 'infinite', and although at first glance the logo looks like a person sitting in meditation, on deeper inspection you can see that the arms reaching upwards also form an eye in the centre. This Mind Calm logo is therefore intended to be a symbolic representation and reminder of the purpose of Mind Calm, which is to be consciously aware by being inwardly attentive to the Infinite I (or 'infinite-eye').

Part I

TEACHINGS + TECHNIQUES

Chapter 1

HIDDEN CAUSES OF A BUSY MIND

Why is my mind soooooooooo busy?!!! I know your frustration. I have felt driven mad by my mind too. Mulling over things at a million miles per hour. I've tossed and turned through sleepless nights, found it near impossible to focus during work or play and, to be totally honest, even had moments when my mind has felt too intense to live with, and secretly questioned whether it wouldn't be easier to check out of this life.

One time I was so caught up in my thoughts I didn't see the wet leaves sprawled across the corner I was heading around and nearly fell off my motorbike. Nearly hitting the hard tarmac that day was certainly a wake-up call, and one of the many motivations that have led to such in-depth exploration into how to move from mental chaos to mind calm.

From this study, together with what I've observed in the many people that I've taught meditation to, I have discovered a number of the subtler hidden causes as to why so many people suffer from such busy minds. I am curious if you can relate to any of them.

THE FOUR HIDDEN CAUSES OF A BUSY MIND + QUICK-START CURES

Hidden cause 1: The Judgement Game

Making sense of life is one of the mind's jobs. Behind the scenes, every moment of every day, your mind is doing its best to attach meaning to everything that happens. With your best interests at heart, it works tirelessly to help you stay safe, keep you on track and have a good life.

Fully committed to this meaning-full role, the mind plays what I call the 'Judgement Game'. With this, your mind judges what has happened in the past, is happening now or might happen in the future. Always with the intention of determining whether it is good or bad, positive or negative, right or wrong, better or worse. Then, if it deems something to be bad, negative, wrong or worse, you end up with what is commonly called a 'problem'.

Judgement and the compulsion to overthink

There is a direct relationship between judging things as being problems and the compulsion to overthink. The mind loves to problem-solve. Having judged something as potentially problematic, it immediately springs into a hive of activity to either produce thoughts about the problem or attempt to find the best possible solutions.

Whether it is a minor irritation or a major catastrophe, the mind tends to react in the same manner: *Why has this happened to me? How might this impact my life? Am I*

4

going to be OK? Is my family going to be OK? How is it making me feel? Why am I feeling this way? How can I change, fix or improve things so everything will be better and I can feel good again?

Usually a deluge of thoughts floods in, as your mind does whatever it can to answer the problem-solving questions that it is truly sublime at creating. Such a stream, or in some cases tsunami, of mental movement stemming from the Judgement Game can be, quite literally, endless! When unintentionally engaged in the Judgement Game, your thoughts can end up going round and round in your mind like a hamster in a turbo-boosted wheel, as you consider the many possible ways to escape your predicament. Quite ironically, all this mental activity happens to be due to the mind's best intentions of bringing resolution, and with it, mind calm.

Improve whatever you want

Let me be clear, there is nothing 'wrong' with making improvements to your life, especially if things are happening that require your attention. You may need to make sure you have enough money to pay the bills this month, do what you can to heal a physical problem or sort a relationship disagreement. However, if you want a calmer mind, to be happier, more loving and tap into your intuition to find creative ways forward then a new relationship with the Judgement Game is required.

Quick cure 1: Suspend judgement

Whether you like it or not, as long as the mind is in play, the Judgement Game will happen. Remember it is how your mind makes sense of reality, which can be very useful at times, especially if potentially life-threatening things are happening. However, if we're completely honest, most things the mind judges and overthinks are not life-threatening at all, far from it. So for the rest of the time – I'd suggest, 99 per cent of the time – it is more useful to suspend judgement.

Suspending judgement requires you to see the judgement instead of being the judger.

The first antidote to this hidden cause for having a chaotic mind is simply to **see it, don't be it**. Shining a light on the judgmental thoughts by seeing them happening in your mind can be incredibly powerful. When you observe the mind, the likelihood of unconsciously reacting to the judgemental opinions is reduced. By seeing the judgement, you can begin to step back from any previous engagement in the destructive game. Instead, you begin to see it for what it is – a judgemental opinion happening in your mind. It can be a remarkable revelation to discover that most of your problems are mind-made and due to an inner judgement of something being bad, negative, wrong or worse.

Albeit a simple strategy, 'seeing the judgement not being the judger' stops you being a victim of circumstance. External people, events or things stop being the cause of your inner stress or lack of serenity. Instead, you see that engaging in the judgements happening in your mind is a major cause of your dissatisfaction with the people, events or things. So whenever you notice that you've been overthinking a problem, take a moment to see the thoughts instead of being the thoughts. Ask this question: *What in my life is my mind currently judging negatively?* Example observations might be:

- I can see that my mind has been judging how much money I have.

- I can see that my mind has been judging what my partner just said to me.

- I can see that my mind has been judging my body.

This is an easy awareness-raising intervention that can create a moment of conscious calm in which you suspend judgement and start to see it for what it is – a thought happening in your mind about life. This insight is made all the more powerful when combined with the next quick cure.

Quick cure 2: It just is!

One of the quickest ways to slow the mind down is to override the Judgement Game with a totally neutral non-opinionated thought. One that is non-judgemental and within it holds the possibility that whatever is happening may not be a problem at all.

> *With no problem needing to be solved, the mind very quickly and naturally becomes still.*

Remember the mind becomes active when it finds a problem that needs to be fixed. But if you are willing to let go of perceiving things as being problems, then you may find your mind has little to do and becomes quiet. Consider: *If something isn't good or bad, right or wrong, better or worse, then 'it just is', right?* Playing with the more neutral opinion that 'it just is', there is very little fuel for the thinking fire. Try it now. Choose a problem from your past, present or future and reflect: *Although this appears to be bad, negative, wrong or worse, I cannot deny the fact that it also just is.*

Having considered this, take a moment to rest without the immediate need to do anything to fix the perceived problem. Take a deep breath in and out, and be attentive to what your mind does next. You may notice that there is a moment of absolute calm as your mind decides its next move. Which, just so you can be prepared, might be another judgement! Your mind might immediately defend its previous position by justifying why the problem is, in fact, bad, negative, wrong or worse.

Whenever you start playing with 'it just is' – be ready for your mind to bring out its big guns, evidence and reasoning! It may want to start defending its previous position by justifying why the problem *is*, in fact, bad, negative, wrong or worse. It might say, *it's a problem because...* and give some reasons why what you're suggesting 'just is' is actually a problem. This is all part of the Judgement Game, so see it, don't be it. The less you engage in the Judgement Game the calmer your mind will be naturally. Waking up to the mind's judgmental tendencies is so vital, as otherwise you'll find it difficult to heal the next hidden cause of having a chaotic mind.

Hidden cause 2: The Resist Persist

Joined at the hip with the Judgement Game is resistance. The mind often starts resisting whatever it has just judged as bad, negative, wrong or worse. Although it may seem natural to push away 'bad' things, moving on, unaware of this hidden cause, leads to a very active mind – due to what happens when you resist things.

Let's have another behind-the-scenes look at the inner workings of the mind. Whenever something happens, your mind immediately jumps into gear – judging whether it is good or bad, positive or negative, right or wrong, or better or worse. We know this by now, but the next unseen habit of the mind is another major cause of overthinking that you must see if you want to be more calm and contented moving forward.

When the mind decides something is good, positive, right and better then it will allow it. This makes sense: it is good, positive, right and better after all! But the game changer that you may not have previously considered is...

It is your optimistic judgements and
subsequent inner allowing of 'what is'
that is the cause of your good feelings.
No person, place or event makes you feel
good, but your inner allowing does.

Take a moment to process this idea. Before, I thought my relationship, money, or new car were the determining factors in making me feel good. In reality, however, it was actually when things happened that my mind judged as good, positive, right or better, that I would allow them to be. I would have a moment of being at peace with 'what is', in which I didn't need my moment to be any different. Or, in other words, I accepted things as they were and had harmony with life in these moments. It turns out, however, that it has always been my allowance of 'what is' that has been the real source of my happiness and contentment. Wow!

The product of pushing life away

However, and it is a big HOWEVER! If your mind judges something as bad, negative, wrong or worse then it is very common for it to start resisting it automatically. Although pushing away negativity may seem both reasonable and logical, it is a major hidden cause of much stress, anguish, heartache and mental chaos.

Prior to exploring the true impact of pushing life events away, I thought it was the people, places, events and things happening that 'made me feel bad'. In reality, however, it was actually my inner mind-made judgements and subsequent resistance that were the cause of all those 'negative' emotions. Quite remarkable really! I spent so many hours working hard to fix, change and improve my body and life so that I could feel good, when all the time my feelings had very little to do with any external factors.

Anger, sadness, fear, guilt, grief, hurt and any other unfavourable feeling you care to mention require negative judgements and resistance in order to exist. Seeing this not only gives you great insight into how to feel fantastic more often – i.e. suspend judgements and remove reactive resistances – but it also shines another illuminating light on how to enjoy more mind calm.

Resistance and the compulsion to overthink

There is a direct relationship between feeling bad due to resisting things and the compulsion to overthink. The mind wants to feel good. In fact, it is the natural tendency of your mind to do whatever it can to help you to be happy. Much of your mind's activity stems from the positive intention to be happy. As a direct consequence, whenever your mind notices what it's learned to be a 'negative' emotional energy, it feels compelled to figure out all possible ways to make the bad feelings go away so you can once again be happy.

Having noticed a negative emotion, two questions usually come to mind:

1.   What am I feeling?

2.   Why am I feeling this way?

Finding the answers to these questions frequently involves lots of mental activity. Once you have given the energy a label – anger, sadness, or anxiety, for example – you will find your mind has a brilliant ability to think up logical and legitimate reasons for why you are feeling the way you do. For example, just a few of the common reasons might be,

•   I'm feeling this way because of what they just said.

•   I'm feeling this way because of the state of my bank account.

•   I'm feeling this way because I'm stuck in this job.

And maybe the other person did say something that was unpleasant to hear, perhaps you are genuinely struggling for cash this month, or you could possibly benefit from moving jobs. But this isn't the point if you want mind calm. More important is to see the mind's hidden causes of overthinking, which happen behind the scenes and are often the source of undesirable feelings. Resisting life won't resolve the relationship disagreement, doesn't help you make more money or make you more effective in getting a new job. Resistance only causes you unnecessary stress and suffering. When you get this, it becomes the obvious choice to let go of resistance and take whatever action is required with mind calm.

Resistance causes stress and suffering.
Acceptance creates calm and is the
more conscious way to live.

Quick cure 1: Remove Reactive Resistance

Lack of money, for example, isn't the cause of bad feelings. Instead, the source of those bad feelings is the mind's judgements and inner resistance to what appears to be happening. If you are willing to play with this possibility then you can be free to feel good now. Worry doesn't help either. In fact, worry involves focusing on the very things you don't want. In short, resistance makes you narrow-minded and magnetizes you to the things you don't want.

By seeing the resistance instead of reactively resisting, the compulsion to overthink about your perceived predicament reduces and is replaced with clear-minded clarity and creativity on ways to improve things. The same is true for any other challenge that you face. Whenever you notice any negative emotions or overthinking about a problem, I recommend you take time out to see the resistance instead of unconsciously resisting. Ask: *What in my life is my mind currently resisting?*

Possible responses might include:

- I can see that my mind is resisting what happened in my past.

- I can see that my mind is resisting my physical condition.

- I can see that my mind is resisting where I'm currently living.

Having identified what you are pushing away, return to having harmony with life by resting instead of resisting. This easy exercise creates a moment of conscious calm. Provided, of course, that you are open to seeing that it is your allowing or resistance that is causing your negative emotions rather than your circumstances. Why intentionally go on resisting life if you know it is your resistance that's making you feel bad? That's not going to help anything because what you resist persists.

> *Resistance only keeps you stuck to what it is you don't want. Instead, let your mind become calm by rising above resistance.*

Quick cure 2: Bring it on!

One very direct way to rise above resistance is simply to say *bring it on* to whatever you happen to be resisting. Simple yes, but powerful, absolutely! Remember: resisting *what is*, is a core, hidden cause of having a hectic mind. Resistance makes your mind mull over the whys, whats, hows and what ifs of the situation – making it very easy to get lost in all of the stories. Whereas saying 'bring it on' to what you're resisting means you can witness something quite remarkable happen: those external forces of circumstance lose their power over your inner experience of life. Amazingly, you can see how they actually needed you NOT to want them, in order to have any authority over your wellbeing. Stop resisting and you immediately feel better.

> *Turn to what it is you think you don't want and welcome it with a wide-open mind.*

Bring it on is a powerful antidote to judgement and resistance. However, again, let me reiterate. I'm not saying you cannot improve things. But instead, the three words 'bring it on' are a determining factor in whether you experience stress, negative emotions and copious amounts of thoughts as you go about changing things, or whether you remain calm.

Hidden cause 3: The Attach Catch

Attachment happens whenever you believe that being, doing or having x, y or z will make you happier, peaceful, loved, successful or some other desirable state. Being attached makes you move away from wanting certain things to believing that you need them to be OK. Attachment is based upon the illusion that you can't feel good now without fixing, changing or improving particular aspects of your body or life first. However, as you've already discovered, feeling calm, content and connected comes from no longer buying into the judgements happening in your mind or resisting life.

Growing up you probably learned what a good life looks like. How much money you should have, the kind of house you should live in, the type of person you should end up with, the shape of body you should have, even the make and model of car you should drive... the list goes on and on.

The criteria for a good life are perpetuated in the movies and media, and can often be unintentionally instilled by our parents and peers. Predictably you can pick up a checklist of requirements in order to enjoy a happy and successful life.

Highly motivated to achieve this good life – as, let's face it, your experience of happiness, peace, love and success depends on it – we take our rulebook of requirements and set about doing everything we possibly can to make it all happen.

I spent countless hours setting goals and working hard to achieve them. Totally lost in a 'I'll be happy when' mentality, I was waiting to feel calm and contented in the future; when I'd ticked off my list everything I thought needed to happen. It was not only tiring but also torturous, especially as I couldn't help noticing how, even when I reached my goals, I only felt good for a short while.

Temporary highs at best

Inadvertently being attached to future outcomes meant that my happiness and peace were only ever fleeting. Whenever I got what I thought I needed, my goalposts would always move to the next big milestone and then the next.

I remember getting into a convertible I'd just bought. Before leaving the showroom, I sat for a few moments looking around at my new purchase. I felt great! Then I looked to my right and noticed a little scratch on the side panel and thought: *Oh well, I'll be happy when I get that fixed!*

Sitting in my expensive convertible, which I'd spent years working to get, my mind gave me about five seconds of pure joy before it found something to judge negatively and resist. Can you relate to this? Without realizing it at the time, I had immediately become attached to the scratch being removed before I could fully enjoy the car again. This is just one example of the many times when I inadvertently fell into what I refer to as the 'Attach Catch'. Caught up in the belief that I couldn't be happy (or some other positive emotion) until certain things in my life were fixed, changed or improved first: *I'll be happy when I get my new home*; *I'll be happy when I've redecorated my new home*; *I'll be happy when I've paid off the mortgage* and so on. Left unseen, the mind can postpone your peace and happiness and be busy forever.

As an aside I still highly recommend goal setting, as having a clear purpose and doing what you enjoy can all help you to make the most of your gift of life. I still have many goals that light me up and drive me forward. I'm not sure if I would spend so many hours writing my books, for example, if I didn't set challenging goals to work towards. However, what is downright destructive to your inner calm is being attached to any of your goals ever happening. Attachment puts your positive feelings on hold until some future date in time and also limits your effectiveness in engaging in life fully.

The Attach Catch gets you totally caught up in the mind, making you miss the present moment, and unnecessarily postpone your peace and prosperity.

Attachment and the compulsion to overthink

There is a direct relationship between being attached to things being a certain way and the compulsion to overthink. Whenever your mind believes that it needs something to be OK, it becomes very active in trying to figure out how to get away from where you are now and into a more appealing time in the future. Attachment dulls your experience of now – the present. It stops the moment you are in ever being good enough, leading to discontentment. Attachment also makes you live in fear. Afraid of people disliking or leaving you, as they are your source of love. Or scared of losing the success you've worked so hard to get. Attachment leads to a very limited life in which you need to control and manipulate things to fit your rulebook of requirements. As a result, the mind is given good cause to start producing copious amounts of thoughts about how to improve your current set of circumstances.

Quick cure: Let go of things needing to be different

Ever catch yourself thinking this classic attachment thought? *I'll be happy when...* Take a moment to consider all the things that you think you need to change, fix or improve before you can be truly happy and enjoy Mind Calm. Whether it is your job, relationship, finances, the healing of a physical condition or something else. Take note of any reasons you can think of for not chilling out and being calm now.

If you feel discontented with any
aspect of your life, then there's a high
chance that you're attached.

Once you have your list, see what happens if you ask this curious question: *What happens within me if I let go of needing this to be any different to how it is now?* Consider it in relation to one or more of the items on your list. Then notice how you feel when you let go of it needing to be fixed, changed or improved? Remember I'm not saying you can't at some point take steps to make things better, but I care most about how you feel right now. **What happens when you let go?**

When I invite my coaching clients and course or retreat participants to do this exercise, I see the same transformations happen time and time again. Common responses are 'I feel relief', 'I feel calm', 'I feel free', along with a range of other really lovely experiences. What happens for you when you are courageously contented? I say courageous because I appreciate it is common not to want to let things be. Your mind may temporarily kick up a fuss that you really must improve things first. It might even tell you that I don't know how bad things are for you, or some other judgement. But if you are willing to be brave, by letting this moment be good enough, exactly as it is, I'm really curious as to what happens inside you.

Hidden cause 4: The Time Trap

Time is a major hidden cause of getting trapped in the mind. When thinking, you are in an imaginary story about something relating to the past and future. You are either thinking about something that's happened in the past, appears to be happening now, or might happen in the future. With an unlimited number of scenarios available to you to get caught up in, you can unwittingly waste years entangled in the time trap.

Going into the past offers, quite literally, a million memories to choose from for as far back as you can remember. Obviously, this can play havoc with your mind calm now if you regularly take jaunts down memory lane (or for some, memory highway!). Not only that, but if you believe in past lives then you can also end up sorting through memories from an infinite supply of other lifetimes, too. Adding to the time trap, you also have the future to contend with, which also brings with it an endless stream of potential scenarios for the mind to become embroiled in. All the time, missing the present moment. The Time Trap, left unseen, makes mind calm near impossible.

Stop thinking and get real

Even thinking about what's happening now is a subtle Time Trap. Incredibly, all of our thoughts are about the past and future. Yes, that's the reality of the situation, every single one! There is no such thing as a present-moment thought. All your thoughts are about the past and future, meaning that if you're thinking, then you will inevitably end up missing the moment you're in.

Although now is the only time anything can happen and so your thoughts are happening now too, the *content* of your thoughts is always about the past and future. Even attempting to think about what's happening now, the moment has always moved on before your mind can process what is happening. To enjoy mind calm and truly experience reality in all its glory, you need to be willing to see when you've left now and gone into an imagined story in your mind. Otherwise you risk spending all your time in your mind.

Time and the compulsion to overthink

There is a direct relationship between believing that the past and future are relevant to your current levels of peace, happiness, love and success and the compulsion to overthink. If you believe that you need to resolve all the 'bad' things that have happened in your life to date, then you will feel compelled to think at length about past memories. Similarly, if you believe that you need to have a better future so you can feel good then, again, you can find yourself needing to engage your mind anytime it presents thoughts about the future, and thinking, for example,

- *What if I run out of money?*

- *What if my body never heals?*

- *What if I never meet anyone?*

- *What if I'm stuck with this person forever?*

Remember, we have a problem anytime we judge and resist 'what is'. Entering the past and future presents your mind with infinite opportunities to judge and resist what's happened in the past or might happen in the future. You can find yourself trapped in judging and resisting made-up future possibilities that haven't even happened. It's such a waste of time! To enjoy mind calm it is vital to accept that whatever's happened in your past or might happen in your future need not have any impact on your current levels of peace.

The only time that you can experience mind calm is now.

When you learn how to be here now, tapping into the inner reservoir of goodness that resides within your current conscious awareness, the lure of leaving your calm consciousness to go into some imagined story in your mind diminishes naturally. You see clearly that now is the only moment you can ever experience clarity, contentment and connection. When you leave now, it feels flat compared to the aliveness of the magnificent moment you are always in.

Quick cure: Reality Check

Escaping the Time Trap involves turning your attention towards now. I'm going to share many ways to do this with you, but one of the simplest is what I like to call having a Reality Check.

Right now, as you read these words, take a moment to notice what you can see – colours, shapes, objects, etc. Now notice what you can hear. Better still, listen for a sound that's been happening but you haven't noticed previously. What sounds can you find in your immediate locality? In order to hear them you need to be really attentive, and thus present. Now, notice what you are physically touching, including the book (or reading device) in your hands, the pressure between your backside and the seat or your feet pressing against the ground. What can you smell or even taste, right now? Totally tune in and have a Reality Check into the immediate here and now.

For a few moments aim to do nothing except be attentive to whatever is being presented to you right now. When doing this, you may notice that your mind becomes stiller. Especially when you give all your attention to what you can see, hear, feel, smell and taste. It can also be fun to see how, in order to re-engage any thoughts, you have to take your attention away from this moment. You will discover later just how important it is to see that shift of attention but, for now, I want to finish this section on the Time Trap by sharing a few words on how to live with time, without being trapped in your mind by it.

It's about time

Obviously, making plans about the future is inevitable and if you never again speak about your past then you might not be the most interesting dinner-party guest! So I want to be clear, I'm not saying you must ignore the past or future. If, however, you continue to ignore the Time Trap then you will find yourself getting lost in your mind, time after time, potentially forever! You will feel compelled to engage with your mind every time it produces thoughts about the past and future. Meaning that Mind Calm will continue to elude you.

With time, you will learn how to talk about the past and future, with your attention firmly rooted in the here and now. You will no longer go into time as you might now. Even if bad things have happened in your past, they won't feel so personal or emotionally intense. You will deeply know that the past is only ever a memory in your mind. That the past or future is not happening at this moment and it is safe and more serene to leave it where it belongs, and make the most of this brand new moment bursting with peace-filled potential.

SUMMARY OF THE FOUR HIDDEN CAUSES

Judgement Game

Judging things as being bad, negative, wrong or worse leads to problems, and the mind becomes very active when attempting to find solutions to problems.

Resist Persist

Resistance to perceived problems leads to stress and suffering. Whenever you feel bad then your mind becomes very active, trying to understand why you feel the way you do and all the ways you can fix, change and improve things so that you can feel good again.

Attach Catch

Believing that x, y or z needs to happen in order to feel good and be successful leads to a busy mind full of thoughts about how to get what you think you need.

Time Trap

Thinking that your past and future determine your current levels of peace, happiness, love and success motivates the mind to produce lots of thoughts about what's happened or might happen.

BE OPEN TO LETTING GO

Can you relate to any of these hidden causes? It is my hope that this chapter has been illuminating for you. So the next time your mind starts playing one of its games, you'll see it and won't feel compelled to take part in its antics. You will find that the less you engage the mind, the less active it will be.

Most importantly, once you see these hidden causes of a busy mind, you'll find it easier to see the mind and not become lost in its inner workings. By being open to letting go of the mind when you see one of these hidden causes, then the big benefits of Mind Calm, which I'll share in the next chapter, will be your reward.

Chapter 2

THE BIG BENEFITS OF MIND CALM

Meditation can benefit anyone who makes it a priority and practises regularly. Over the past few years of teaching people from all backgrounds, I haven't met a single person who hasn't ended up benefiting from adopting a meditation routine.

Stepping back from the rigmarole of daily duties, taking a break from overthinking about the rights and wrongs of life, and scheduling in regular time-outs to close your eyes to enjoy stillness is a marvellous gift you can give yourself. Time after time, meditators experience less stress, better health, inner calm, clarity and creativity, more loving relationships and even increased productivity.

A PERPLEXING OBSERVATION

Despite meditation having such big benefits, it is quite remarkable that so few people actually do it. Having taught meditation around the world I've been fascinated to hear the many reasons people come up with as to why they don't meditate, including:

- 'I can't do it.'

- 'It's difficult.'

- 'It's boring.'

- 'I don't have time.'

- 'I always fall asleep.'

- 'It's scary.'

- 'It's religious.'

- 'It's satanic.' (Yes, I've honestly been told this!)

- 'It's only for "tree-hugger" types.'

The list goes on...

Can you relate to any of these? As you continue reading, I'm confident that if you have indeed resonated with any of these reasons then you will see that they aren't true. Furthermore, having touched upon the common reasons for not meditating, the purpose of this chapter is to outline some of the big benefits possible from adopting a regular meditation routine, so that you are more motivated to meditate with the Mind Calm techniques shared later in the book.

10 BIG BENEFITS OF MEDITATION

Benefit 1: From stress to serenity

Imagine a bathtub with a shower over it. Throughout your day the water is running, filling the bathtub. In this analogy, the bath is your body–mind and the water is stress. As you go about your day without meditation, the running water (stress) fills the bathtub (your body–mind). For some, this stress-filled scenario can happen day in day out for decades. Closed-eye meditation is the equivalent of pulling the plug out of the bathtub and draining the water (stress). As you sit and use the Mind Calm techniques that I'll teach you later in the book, stress is released from your body. This is a completely natural process, just as when the body rests it tends to take the opportunity to let go of stored-up stress.

When combined with open-eye meditation throughout your day, it is like turning down the water to a reduced rate of flow. Engaging life from a more meditative state of mind, you become Teflon-coated, as less stress sticks to your body–mind. As a result, less stress is accrued. As you can appreciate, used together, closed- and open-eye meditation can play a big role in massively reducing the stress borne by your body, and bring with it an enhanced serenity and wellbeing.

Benefit 2: Sleep without counting sheep

Using meditation as you fall asleep at night can help you enter sleep at a deeper level and experience a better quality of rest. Personally, I used to need my eight hours of sleep every night or I would end up exhausted. However, these days I meditate throughout the day with my eyes open (see 'Calm Moments' page 95), and also meditate as I fall asleep at night. With this powerful combination I find that I don't need as many hours as I used to in order to feel full of energy the next day. This is a great way to save time and get more done during my day, but as an added benefit my relationship with sleep has improved.

Before, if I wasn't tired or couldn't get to sleep, I would lie awake worrying about how tired I would be the next day. Now, knowing that my body and mind get huge rest from meditation, I lie in bed meditating. Sometimes I fall asleep and other times I have an amazingly clear and calm meditation. Irrespective of what happens, knowing meditation rests my body and mind has liberated me from worrying about whether I'm getting enough sleep or not. So there's no need to count any more sheep to get to sleep; instead, you can gently drift off into the best night's rest with meditation.

Benefit 3: Helping hand to heal

Two of the most widely proven strategies for aiding physical healing, discovered by the scientific community and regularly recommended by modern medical professionals, have also been practised for thousands of years by ancient civilizations and are simply:

1.   Reduce stress
2.   Increase rest

They are also, as you've just learned, two of the major benefits from regular meditation. If you see your medical practitioner, you may get a diagnosis or a prescription medicine, but more often than not you will be recommended to go home and 'get some rest'. This is because the body heals best when it rests.

Prolonged chronic stress can lead to living in a perpetual state of fight or flight. In such a state, assimilation, digestion and elimination of food is compromised, along with many of the maintenance and repair projects undertaken by the body when at rest or sleep. By taking time out to meditate, you dramatically improve the physical functioning of your body and, in turn, promote your immune system and aid the healing of any physical conditions that require attention.

Benefit 4: Calm + contentment

Angst, unease and discontentment are common by-products of a busy mind and, as you've already discovered, resistance to life is one of the most common hidden causes of an array of 'negative' emotions. Meditation can help you rise above resistance and cultivate a healthier habit of acceptance. Through regular practice, you learn to let go of having to fix, change, improve, manage and manipulate everything in accordance with how your mind believes it needs to be for you to be OK. You start to find that you can let things be. You can change what you want, but don't need to resist life, throw a tantrum if things don't go your way or force your opinions onto others or life. You ultimately learn through your experience that the less you resist life, the more peace you naturally enjoy. It becomes the obvious choice to let things be.

Resistance  Mind Calm

Contentment is also a common by-product of the move away from resistance. You discover that discontentment happens whenever you find fault and want the moment you're in to be different in some way or another. You see that discontentment can creep into your experience of life if you are focusing too much on the gap between where you are now and where you would rather be. With meditation you can find yourself appreciating what you already have, and as a natural consequence, feel more contented with the way things are, right now.

Benefit 5: Unconditional confidence

Low self-esteem and a lack of confidence are often the result of relying too heavily on the opinions of your mind and/or others. People experiencing low confidence can overly compare themselves to others, find fault in their current incarnation and wish they were different, better or improved.

Meditation helps you to move your attention away from the opinionated voice in your head. You no longer rely on, or need to wait for, your mind to tell you when you are deemed good enough. Instead, you accept the person you are now – warts and all. As you move into a more unconditional acceptance of yourself, you let go of conceptual criteria-based: *I'm good enough and loveable because x, y or z*. Naturally your levels of self-love increase along with your confidence and belief in your abilities.

Furthermore, as you learn to rest more into the gentle yet powerful permanent presence of your being, to your delight, you can discover that the essence and direct experience of your being is love. This love is beyond the mind and therefore beyond conditions. It is a beautiful peace-filled calm that exists within you. Within everyone! Irrespective of body shape or weight, career success or any other external gauge that you have previously used to determine if you were good enough to be loved. You can deeply know that you are, and meditation can once and for all reveal this undeniable truth.

Benefit 6: Deeply loving relationships

As within as without, as the gentler, more accepting and loving that you are towards yourself, so naturally you project your inner experience outwards and become gentler, more accepting and loving of the other people in your life too.

Until you find love within yourself it can put a massive pressure on any relationship, especially intimate ones. If the other person is the source of your love, then there can be an attachment to them being a certain way for you to feel loved. Holding on and grasping can occur as you see them as the source of your love. If they go, so does love. In these sorts of love-dependent relationships, fear is prevalent. One or both parties are scared of the other person leaving and taking their love away. 'I love you' is often said, not as a heart-based expression of love, but more for the person saying it to hear it back.

Relationships are the ultimate mirror. As you criticize yourself less, the less you need to criticize others. The less you judge yourself, the less you judge others. The more harmony you find within, the more harmony you find in your relationships. The more at peace you are within yourself, the less you need to fix, change and manage other people in your life, so that they fit with your ideas, expectations and fear-based needs. You don't need anyone to 'complete' you as you experience yourself as a complete being, lacking nothing.

Meditation can also cause the old mind-made constructs of separation and dualism to fall away, revealing an experience of oneness. You see that to harm another person is really to harm yourself. The more intimate you become with your Self (the love-filled presence of your being), the more intimate and deeper loving relationships you experience with others.

Benefit 7: Live in the magnificent moment

There is no such thing as a present-moment thought. Being caught up in your mind entangles you in the Time Trap. You end up thinking about the past and future and miss the magnificent moment you're in now. But when the attraction to engaging with thoughts and thinking diminishes, you naturally become more aware of now. The more you become consciously aware, the more you become aligned with the aspect of your real Self that is already always present. Better still, you discover that when you are consciously aware of now, you naturally hang out in the inner peace that's always present within you.

Thinking takes you into the past and future.

Meditation brings you back to the here and now.

Benefit 8: Eradicate excessive thinking

Over time, perhaps ironically, you will see that being present is much more enlivening and appealing than being lost in mind-made stories. You see that when you're overthinking, you are missing the remarkable reality of now, and caught up in resistance, judgement, attachment, the past and future. More importantly, when you stop trying to fix all the woes of life, you are able to enjoy life and the fixes follow naturally.

One of the purposes of meditation is to be able to stop thinking and return to present-moment awareness. When you begin a regular meditation practice, you may find that you continue to get caught up in the thinking mind, but as you gain experience, you'll get bored of the stories and your desire to defend its dramas naturally diminishes.

Although you may think that the exploits of the mind have been giving meaning to your life, you see it becomes even more meaningful and magical when you have woken up from incessant thinking. Attuned to the present, you are able to engage life with calm and clear attentive awareness. Obviously, there will be times when you fall into habitual thinking but, when you notice that you've been lost in your mind, it then becomes the obvious choice to be here now and conscious, not wasting time mulling over problems and scenarios created by your mind.

Benefit 9: Perform at your best

Mind Calm makes you more productive, able to perform at your absolute best. When you are too busy thinking, you end up distracted from the task in hand, getting stressed about the long list of things needing to be done, and lacking the ability to make creative decisions and take concise actions. Being present with a clear mind allows you to give all of your attention to whatever you are working on and, when you are done, then leave it in the past to progress with the next task and the next. Irrespective of the workload there is very little stress when working this way, as life only becomes stressful when you leave the now and start thinking about all the things that need to be done.

The reality is, you can only ever do very little in the immediate moment you're in. For example, right now you can only read the word in front of you. However, if you start thinking about how you are going to find the time to finish the book, it is not only distracting but also makes your journey towards your goals more stress-filled. By giving what you're doing now your fullest undivided attention, you will get more done and at a far superior standard. Not only that, but you will be delighted to discover that even when faced with high demands, you can remain calm and focused throughout.

Benefit 10: Liberation from limitations

Finally, and perhaps most wonderfully, meditation leads to a more liberated way of living. Effortlessly, you find that you don't need to control your thoughts, emotions, body and life in order to attain the peace, love, joy and fulfilment you want. In fact, you recognize that the best way to enjoy all these great states of being is to let go of control and go with the flow. You can still get lots done and make any changes you may want, but you become less resistant to life and engage less with the mind-based judgemental thinking that may have previously talked you out of feeling good along the way.

Attachment falls away as you no longer need your life to be any certain way for you to be happy. Your mind has less fuel for the thinking fire and instead you are filled with the awe and wonder of the present moment as it reveals an inner sense of freedom that is immensely fulfilling.

SUMMARY OF THE 10 BENEFITS OF MEDITATION

1. From stress to serenity

2. Sleep without counting sheep

3. Calm + contentment

4. Helping hand to heal

5. Unconditional confidence

6. Deeply loving relationships

7. Live in the magnificent moment

8. Eradicate excessive thinking

9. Perform at your best

10. Liberation from limitations

Chapter 3

WHAT YOU WANT IS INSIDE YOU

What do you want more than anything else? Having read through some of the big benefits possible from meditation, which of them stand out as your must-haves? I cannot recommend highly enough the life-changing importance of gaining clarity on your heart's highest hope. Without knowing the answer to the aforementioned question, you can end up wasting vast amounts of time, energy and effort looking for what you want in places where it can't be found.

Instead, by shining a light on your most important gains from meditation, you will dramatically increase both your commitment and motivation to meditate. You will also be able to adopt the most effective strategy to move towards your heart's highest hope, rather than busily work away hoping for the best. When combined, the right commitment, motivation and strategy add up to the formula you need for making success unavoidable.

GET CLEAR NOW.
If you had a magic wand and could have any one wish, what would you ask for?

Having asked this question to thousands of people around the world, I've been fascinated to observe the same answers coming up time and time again:

- Peace

- Happiness

- Contentment

- Truth

- Joy

- Confidence

- Love

- Freedom

THE DIFFERENCE BETWEEN WHAT + HOW

Occasionally people will initially say they want more money or better health. What's interesting about these answers is how, when asked why they want these things, it is usually fuelled by the belief that things like money or health will make them happier, peaceful or more loved. So by that rationale, it means they, too, ultimately want peace, love or happiness or some other positive state of being.

When wanting money or health, the person is usually focusing more on **how** they can get what they ultimately want, rather than **what** they actually want. Get the difference? This shift between focusing on **what** instead of **how** can be the difference between hoping to feel good one day and enjoying what you want now.

So **what** do you want, more than anything else?

Gaining clarity on understanding that what you want is an inner experience, rather than external things like money, the perfect partner or a fancy car, is also a liberating realization, because then most people finally understand why they haven't been experiencing it up until now.

LOOKING OUTSIDE FOR INNER EXPERIENCES

In the pursuit of peace, happiness, love and other appealing states, it is easy in today's media-driven world to fall into the trap of believing these inner experiences are the result of changing, improving and perfecting our physical body or circumstances. However, looking outside your Self for positive inner experiences postpones peace, breeds discontentment and limits love.

It is how you believe things will make you feel on the inside that makes you want to pursue getting them.

How often, for example, have you thought?

- I will be able to relax when I get everything done.

- I will experience love when I meet my soul mate.

- I will feel successful when I get the promotion.

Thinking you need to have a big house, fancy car, prestigious career, bulging bank account, social significance and the right relationships are the main causes of unhappiness and discontentment on the planet. Yes, these things are nice to have and can at times make life a bit easier, but to enjoy mind calm sooner rather than later it might be time to explore the possibility that these external things don't need to have any relationship with how good you feel on the inside.

Peace, love, happiness and contentment are the natural by-product of having a harmonious relationship with life.

I mentioned earlier that I used to believe that getting the car, the bigger house, the special relationship or whatever, was the source of my happiness and a prerequisite to peace. However, in reality I was living an illusion. The truth is that we feel good when we attain goals because it temporarily satisfies the mind with the way things are in the present. The feel-good feelings are the result of taking time out from negatively judging, and resisting the present moment due to getting what we wanted.

WAITING FOR HAPPY EVER AFTER

Looking to gain serenity from life's circumstances leads to only fleeting moments of peace, love or happiness because careers, relationships, finances and all other aspects of life are in a constant state of flux and change. Yes, you might finally get the car you've always wanted and feel good, but what happens when the new make or model is released? If you are relying on the new car as your source of happiness, then suddenly the car you've got can become less desirable and discontentment can creep in. Or you might secure the big promotion, but then you need to deal with the new responsibilities and longer working hours or spend more time away from your family, for example.

In short, it is a risky and often ineffective strategy to pin your hopes for happiness on external things that come and go. So is it all bad news? Should you give up on your goals? Not at all!

YOU ARE WHAT YOU WANT

The great news is that your consciousness is already filled with peace and love, is constantly content and beyond words brilliant. It's never sick, doesn't have a bad day, become faulty, get upset, worry or fear for its survival. It's beyond all of that. It's beyond the mind, beyond emotions, beyond the body, beyond your life circumstances. Aware of it all happening, it is a calm companion that you can totally rely on to always be with you, hold you and be a constant reminder that all is well. Yes, all is very well. Nothing is wrong with you; your conscious awareness is perfect, whole and complete.

By rediscovering the aspect of you that is consciously aware, you experience the essence of your being. It has been said that you are a human being, not a human doing. It is so easy to forget this undeniable truth; to be distracted by doing loads of stuff to try to make your mind happy, enjoy some peace and have a good life. So much energy, time and attention expended in the never-ending pursuit of happy ever after. The place you really want to get to is here and now. The person you really want to be is who you are right now. They say home is where the heart is, and when you're consciously aware you naturally become present and fully turn up and play big in whatever you do.

Sound good? In the spirit of no longer waiting until things are better, fixed, changed or improved, in the next chapter you'll discover that what you want is inside you, when I share one of my favourite techniques for getting mind calm now.

Chapter 4

QUICK START: GET MIND CALM NOW

Mind Calm is quicker and easier than you may think! Thinking occurs when you engage in the flow of thoughts happening in your mind. When you are thinking, you have essentially fallen asleep. You are no longer awake to the present moment reality and are distracted by an imagined mind-made version of yourself and life. The habits of the thinking mind mean that you will very likely find yourself preoccupied by one or more of the hidden causes of a chaotic mind outlined in Chapter 1 (see page 3). Whereby you will be caught up in judgement, resistance and/or attachment, and spending time in the past or future.

- Ultimate hidden cause: unconscious thinking
- Ultimate mind calm cure: conscious awareness

The more you think, the more you will be compelled to think. It's as simple as that. The more you judge and resist life the more you will feel compelled to find solutions to all the problems that your mind has conjured up. So, as long as you continue to fall into unconscious thinking, your mind will gather momentum for further thinking. Tragically for some people this unfortunate cycle of perpetually thinking up new problems to solve can last a lifetime. They are never able to enjoy the pure peace that comes from being present and awake through being consciously aware. They constantly search for peace by perfecting their life on the outside, forever missing the inner calm that lives within them. For you, my hope is that you once and for all call an end to the endless stream of incessant thinking by actively playing with what I affectionately call GAAWO.

GENTLY ALERT ATTENTION WIDE OPEN (GAAWO)

By far the easiest and quickest way to bring an end to the cycle of incessant thinking and allow your mind to become calm is by being consciously aware. When you are consciously aware you naturally step back from engaging in the mind and return to the still silent spacious aspect of yourself that is already calm. I'm going to talk much more about this in later chapters, but for now, my priority is for you to start exploring it without any more concepts to cloud your innocent experience.

'Meditation is active calmness.'
PARAMAHANSA YOGANANDA

When engaging GAAWO you naturally become consciously aware. In doing so, marvellous things happen. Your mind immediately becomes quieter or, dare I say it, silent. When using GAAWO you may notice that there are literally no thoughts happening. Consequently, there will be no judgement, nothing to resist, no attachment, and no concept of time. You find yourself right here, right now. Naturally experiencing what it is like to live in a 'bring it on, it just is, let it go' state of being. You will find that there is no reason not to feel calm and content as you continue to be gently alert with your attention wide open. Sound good? Let's play!

How to engage GAAWO

Looking at this page, as you continue to read the words in front of you, relax your gaze and let your field of vision spread out to the left and right. Do not look directly at anything to your left and right. Instead use your peripheral vision simply to notice what is there. You may not be able to see it all clearly or with sharp focus, so it might be blurred. That's OK. Your intention right now is to gently let your attention open up wide to the left and right as you continue to look ahead at the words on the page.

Now, as you do this, notice what it's like to let your attention open up wide, both upwards and downwards. In your peripheral vision you might be able to see your lap and the colour of the clothes you are wearing. Above you might see the ground beyond the book and/or the wall as it extends upwards to meet the ceiling (if you're inside somewhere). Irrespective of where you are or what you can see, just gently let your attention open up wide to notice what you can see both above and below the page. What is it like to be gently alert with your attention wide open? What's happening in your mind? Is it chaotically busy or calm and quiet? Has your inner experience of this moment become more restful? Can you notice an inner spaciousness or even stillness present, as you engage GAAWO now?

When you gently engage GAAWO, you naturally disengage the mind.

TOP TIP: JUST DO IT!

Thinking about GAAWO and actively engaging GAAWO are two different things with very different results. GAAWO will work if you just do it. Avoid over-analysing. Jump into the experience and observe what happens inside your mind, body and consciousness.

With your attention resting wide open, what it is like to do absolutely nothing, except be gently attentive to everything that's being presented to you, right now?

One of the exciting observations you might notice is that you have to disengage GAAWO in order to start thinking again. Or, put another way, you might find that if you've start thinking you probably won't have been actively employing GAAWO. This includes thinking about whether or not GAAWO is working for you. So be alert to that subtle shift in where your attention is placed, including the mind's habitual tendency to jump into judgement. If you're not conscious of your focus moving away from GAAWO, then you can immediately drop into judgement again and conclude that GAAWO is ineffective. It's not. I've found it to work for everyone who uses it as taught.

The first step of Mind Calm meditation

Perhaps one of the most appealing features of Mind Calm is that you can use it with your eyes open or closed. When you use Mind Calm you will start by engaging GAAWO. So play with GAAWO as you read on and in between times when you're getting on with other things. There is more to Mind Calm than GAAWO, but using it now is a brilliant quick start to creating the new habit of calm and will make what you'll learn later much easier.

I ♥ GAAWO!

One of my favourite aspects of my work is when I first introduce people to what happens when they are gently alert with their attention wide open. Looking into their eyes as they engage GAAWO I see a calm peace emerge from within them, and more often than not a smile appears on their face. There is something so exciting and precious about the moment when a person realizes they have a tool to attain mind calm in moments, whenever they choose.

FROM MIND CALM TO MIND MASTERY

Knowing how to calm the chaotic mind is often a turning point in many people's lives. My hope is that everyone, both young and old, can be empowered with this ability. Saying that, I also want people to experience true Mind Mastery, which is beyond solely having the ability to stop the mind. Instead Mind Mastery occurs when you engage with your mind and use it as the incredible tool that it is, and then let it go when you want to return to calmness.

In fact, focusing on shutting the mind up is very much missing the point. It is not Mind Mastery. At best it is mind manipulation. Aiming to push the mind away often requires there to be a part of you that is concerned about what your next thought or feeling might be. A part of you that is busy trying to keep the mind happy. This part of you is also your mind, by the way! The mind can be scared of its own shadow, as it produces thoughts about thoughts all day. That's not freedom, quite the opposite. What a waste of time and energy, and what a missed opportunity to experience the fullness of what it means to be born human. The mind can be an amazing ally for you. You can use it to achieve incredible things for yourself, and bring immense good into the lives of others and the planet.

A STRATEGY FOR LIBERATED LIVING

The aim is to live a liberated life where you no longer need to push away any aspect of the human experience. You were born with a mind and it exists for good and beneficial reasons. God (or whatever you prefer to call the Divine) didn't perfect the planets, nature, biology and your soul and then run out of steam and make a mistake with your mind. It is not that your mind is bad; it is only that your relationship with your mind can become imbalanced if you lose sight of calm consciousness. Separation is an illusion. The concept of having a mind, body and soul is just that – a mental construct. Nothing is separate; every 'part' of you exists within supreme consciousness. To resist your mind is to push away an aspect of yourself fully deserving of love, too.

Stop rejecting your mind as if it were an ugly duckling; instead rediscover the majestic swan of conscious awareness.

More useful is learning how to befriend your mind and not take it so seriously when it takes jaunts down not so positive avenues. Engage with your mind when it's useful, and be willing and able to let it go to return to still calm consciousness whenever its work is done. Cultivating this kind of liberated, loving and resourceful relationship with your mind requires a new strategy. Instead of having to tame it, change it so it is only positive. Fix it so it has no undesirable facets and make it go away so you can enjoy some peace. I'm now going to share a new way of relating to your mind that will dramatically improve the quality of life, for good.

Chapter 5

THE PEACE WITH MIND MIRACLE

'Peace of mind' is perhaps one of the most confusing terms used by the mainstream media and in spiritual circles today. Mainly owing to all the unhelpful images it conjures up, often including robe-clad monks sitting in full lotus with a serene look on their faces. Why so serene? It's easy to assume they have achieved an empty mind, devoid of thoughts or emotions. Making peace of mind for many living busy lives in today's modern techno-deadline-driven-highly-stimulated world, a pipe dream at best.

THE PEACE OF MIND MYTH

How many thoughts would you say you have every day? If you've been drawn to read this book then there's a high chance you're already aware that the number runs into thousands. Although the figures vary, the average person has as many as 100,000 thoughts every day – about a thought a second. Wow, no wonder you bought this book! Perhaps more worryingly, though, is having taught meditation around the globe, I'd say it is an underestimation to suggest that at least half of these thoughts are of a negative nature. That works out at a staggering 50,000 negative thoughts every day.

By proposing this I don't mean to offend anyone, especially those who have undertaken self-improvement to think positively. But if you are ruthlessly honest with yourself, you might find a large proportion of your thoughts are less than 100 per cent positive in nature. And you'd be right to think so, as these statistics make sense when you remember that the mind operates using the Judgement Game – putting everything that has happened, is happening or might happen into mind-made boxes of good or bad, positive or negative, right or wrong, better or worse. No wonder so many people end up having 'negative' thoughts now and again.

NEGATIVE THOUGHTS ARE INEVITABLE

With a desire to keep you safe and help you to be happy, it is natural for your mind to consider all the possible worst-case scenarios that could happen. It does so with your best interests at heart. Mainly so you can be fully prepared in advance for any and all potentially negative eventualities.

> *Negative thoughts are actually positively intended.*

Taking account of these facts and figures, relating to the quantity of thoughts and the mechanics of the mind, it makes the quest of mastering 'positive thinking' by only having positive thoughts a massive and potentially impractical task. So if you've tried to master positive thinking but still find negative thoughts popping in, be easy on yourself. You're not failing as a human being by having negative thoughts. Instead you've just been attempting to achieve a positive pipe dream, which is not only against the natural tendencies of the mind but also a mammoth task owing to the sheer quantity of negative thoughts occurring each day.

So is it a lost cause? Should you just give up trying to be positive? Not necessarily! Occasionally focusing on positive thoughts can be very useful, especially when it comes to having a healthy body and achieving your goals. However, when it comes to enjoying mind calm together with more ongoing serenity and success, I would like to offer a practical strategy that works with the natural tendency of your mind, rather than against it.

IT'S YOUR RELATIONSHIP WITH THOUGHTS THAT COUNTS

Improving your relationship with your mind, so you can be at peace with whatever thoughts pass through your conscious awareness, is possible. Furthermore, learning to let your thoughts come and go from a more neutral viewpoint can be very liberating indeed.

Being at peace with your mind makes it feasible to maintain a state of calm contentment, even when negative thoughts are occurring in your mind. For example, this thought might pop into your mind: *What if I run out of money this month*? If you don't see the thought and let it go as fast as it came, you can end up resisting the thought. As a result, you can end up experiencing an array of emotions, including angst or fear, as the feelings associated with resisting the thought flood your body–mind. However, if you can see the thought – by being consciously aware – you will find that the thought can be present within you without it being a problem or causing you any stress whatsoever. What a relief!

Life can become an emotional roller coaster if you fully engage in every thought that passes through your mind. Seeing your thoughts instead of being your thoughts makes all the difference.

Being consciously aware is paramount to how you relate to your mind. Remember, you are that which is aware of your mind. Meaning if you are unaware then you are more likely to engage in a negative thought, and get lost in unproductive downward-spiralling thinking and feeling. If, however, you can be aware enough to observe your thoughts then it creates some space between you and the thoughts, and you simultaneously experience the inner calm of your conscious awareness.

To illustrate this point, let's do a quick experiment. Stop reading for a moment and look at the next page.

OK, so once you have looked at the page, I'd like you to consider this question: *What were you immediately aware of the most?* Would you say your attention went mainly to:

1. the bird in the centre of the page, or

2. the blank space everywhere else on the page?

Despite this being an incredibly simple exercise, it shines a light on where you might be habitually putting your attention most, and thus how you currently relate to your mind, emotions and life in general.

Most people say their attention naturally focuses on A – the bird in the centre of the page – but in doing so, they are unaware of the blank space all around. This was true for me, too, the first time I did this experiment. So if your attention also went to the bird then you are not alone. We are so accustomed to putting our attention on the most obvious content that we unintentionally miss the context (more about this in Chapter 6, see page 63). Plus, this common habit of focusing on the content means we inadvertently end up missing more than we could possibly imagine.

But before I get into what exactly, let's take our bird analogy off the page and up into the sky. I want you to imagine that you are outside on a summer's day looking up at the big blue sky. That day there isn't a cloud to be seen from horizon to horizon. You find yourself sitting enjoying the vast vista that extends as far as you can see. That day the bigness of the sky is awe-inspiring. Taking it all in (with your attention wide and open) you feel calm, as you rest back attentive to the stunning still sky. Then, out of the blue, a bird flies across your field of vision. Upon noticing the bird, you take your attention away from the sky and place it all on the bird as it flies on by.

After a few moments of tracking the bird across the sky, you start wondering what type of bird it is, why it's there, where it's headed and why it's alone. Engaging in thoughts about the bird, you stop feeling as calm as you did when your full attention was on the sky. Instead you start feeling your thinking that's started happening in your mind about the bird.

Nice story, yes, but the practical implications of this little analogy are IMMENSE when it comes to mind calm. Allow me to hazard a guess that the exact same scenario is actually happening within you, too. Obviously you might not think much about birds, unless you're a birdwatcher, of course. But inside you now there exists a vast sky of light-filled conscious awareness with thoughts and emotions (birds) flying around within it.

If, out of habit – and because we aren't usually taught a better alternative while growing up – you've been missing mind calm, then you will have been putting most of your attention on your thoughts, instead of the conscious awareness that's aware of your thoughts. Or said slightly differently, you have been putting most of your attention on what you are aware of, instead of what is aware. In doing so, you've been missing the still silent spacious conscious awareness that is inherently peace-filled.

Now here's the really cool question: In the case of this sky-bird analogy, just because you might have all of your attention on the bird, does it mean the sky stops existing?

Of course not! Similarly, just because you've had all of your attention on your thoughts and emotions, it doesn't mean that your calm conscious awareness has ever stopped being present within you either. It just means that you may not have noticed it, yet!

PEACE IS AWARE OF YOUR MIND

With all of your attention placed firmly on all of the movement happening in your mind, you can end up unaware of the calm conscious awareness that's watching all of the mental and emotional activity. Consequently you can end up walking around with peace built into the fabric of your being, but miss it your entire life. What a tragic predicament!

What if you've been looking for calm by stopping or changing your thoughts and emotions when, all the time, the consciousness that is aware of your mind is already as calm as calm can be? Without waking up to this liberating possibility, you could spend years searching for peace in places it simply cannot be found.

Looking for calm by stopping your thoughts is a bit like looking for a winning lottery ticket in filing cabinet A when all the time it's sitting in filing cabinet B. You can look all you like, put filing cabinet A into perfect order and even invest in some nice shiny solid gold dividers, but if your winning lottery ticket isn't in the drawer you're looking in then it doesn't matter how long you search, as you obviously won't find it. The same is true for peace, happiness, love and true success. So, perhaps it's time to stop looking for these things by getting rid of your negative thoughts and emotions, or by attempting to perfect your body or life.

The consciousness that's aware of it all is already perfectly calm and the source of truly abundant living.

> *You don't need to try to get peace by having no thoughts because the still silent conscious awareness that's aware of your thoughts is already peace-filled.*

PEACE WITH LIFE LIBERATION

Growing up I was constantly learning how life worked. For example, anytime my mum seemed to be having a bad day, appearing frustrated or unhappy, I'd often hear the same few words come out of her mouth: 'If I was just a size 12 again then I'd be happy.' Quite inadvertently, observing my mother I ended up picking up the belief: *For me to be happy, my body must be perfect.*

Fast forward a few years to my late-teens, and I had times when I didn't feel secure or happy within myself. Assuming my body was the cause of my discomfort, off I trotted to the nearest gym to start pumping iron. After a few months of working out almost every day, I remember looking into the mirror and, despite a rather pumped physique being reflected back, I wasn't happy yet. So I concluded that it must be due to something else: *My skin is the wrong colour.* I'm not kidding! So, I started using a sunbed to tan my body with the hope that I'd finally feel good. It didn't work!

> *I thought I was my body so assumed changing it would make me feel more loveable and happy.*

'Peace with body' is possible because you are not your body. Instead you are that which is aware of your body. If you were to lose the end of your little finger, would you be less of you or would you have less of a body? You would be fully intact (your real Self that is). Your body would just be missing a bit. The permanent consciousness that resides partly within the temporary body constantly changes, eventually gets old and returns to the earth. By becoming more consciously aware, you can rest within the aspect of you that never gets sick, fat or skinny, or dies. Consciousness is beyond the physical body and therefore mind calm is possible, irrespective of the weight, shape or health of your physical body.

Getting peace with your body is just one example of how you can transform your relationship with life in general. By getting peace with your thoughts about your relationships, career, finances, living conditions and so on, you can be calm and contented irrespective of how these individual elements of your life happen to be. Instead of having individually to fix, change or improve your life, you can totally eradicate the sense that something is wrong. By adopting my 'peace with' strategy to be at peace with your emotions, your body, your relationships, your career and so on, you can engage life in a liberated way, free from fear and full of courageous contentment and clarity.

THE 'PEACE WITH MIND' MIRACLE

Looking for peace in your mind (by having no thoughts), in your emotions (by only feeling positive), in your physical body (by it being healthy and looking how you think it should) or in your career, money, relationships or any other aspects of your external life circumstances does not work. You don't need to take my word for it; your life experiences can be evidence enough. So, if you haven't found mind calm or true fulfilment by trying to change, improve and perfect your body, your mind or your life, it's probably time for a new strategy.

The miraculous fact that your conscious awareness is already inherently still, silent and peaceful means you don't need to stop your thoughts in order to experience calm. Instead you just need to learn how to be at peace with your thoughts about your body and life through being inwardly attentive to your conscious awareness. With the Mind Calm meditation and Peace with Mind Protocol shared in the next couple of chapters, you'll learn how to do this by being consciously aware in daily life. But, before I teach you the full methods, I'm going to prepare you further by making you more willing to release your grasp on the mind. To do this, I want you to see why there is so much more to life than you think...

Chapter 6

THE SECRET TO SUCCESS IS STILLNESS

On the surface, success appears to mean different things for different people. For some it might be optimum health, while others associate success with financial wealth or reaching the top of their organization or profession. Irrespective of your personal benchmark on what a successful life looks like, without discovering the inner presence of stillness, experiencing success in life can end up only ever being fleeting and often lack lasting satisfaction.

Despite accumulating possessions and prestige, the nagging sense that there's more to life can continue. Mainly because, without knowing inner stillness, you are missing a huge aspect of your Self and life that no set of circumstances can satisfy.

Like the surface of the ocean, your thoughts, emotions, body, career, relationships, finances and all other aspects of your external world are constantly changing. That's what they do. Thoughts and emotions happen, while the body does its thing. New people enter your life as others leave. Careers change, political parties rise and fall and economic climates change as quickly as the weather. Owing to all these aspects of your body, your mind and your life being in a constant state of flux, ebbing and flowing between what the mind deems as being good or bad, up and down, it is no wonder you don't find much long-lasting serenity or success by attempting to find it in the transient movement of life.

On your quest for success, I'm excited to now share my 'Content–Context' model, which illustrates why living a truly successful life only really becomes possible when you get to know the stillness within your abundant consciousness. It is my hope that you clearly see the choice that must be made moving forward, if you want to step beyond surface-level success to enjoy genuine and lasting deep satisfaction in business and life.

THE CONTENT–CONTEXT MODEL

My explorations into finding true serenity and success within this lifetime have included meditating day and night for many months. During these extended periods of meditation and, of course, my daily meditation routine, I've discovered that this Content–Context model offers a roadmap for finding freedom from mind-made problems and enjoying what can best be described as heaven on earth – in which you experience life in its perfection.

With exquisite simplicity, this model explains how the quality of your life ultimately comes down to where you put your attention in any given moment, and specifically whether your attention rests on:

- the **content** of your life, or

- the **context** of your life.

In a bid to bring the Content–Context model to life for you, let's take the room you're currently in as an example. There might be furniture, flowers, light fittings, your telephone and other belongings. The term I use to refer to all these things is STUFF. Now, for all the stuff to exist, there has to be the context of SPACE. In fact, there has to be more space than stuff, otherwise the stuff wouldn't fit into the space. And although the stuff will eventually come and go, the space that it inhabits is constant, ever-present and unchanging.

Content	Context
Stuff	Space

Continuing to read these words you may become aware of SOUNDS around you. There might be a clock ticking, birds singing, the hum of traffic in the distance, the shimmering of leaves outside your window, music playing or people talking nearby. For these sounds to exist, indeed for you to hear anything, they have to happen within a context of SILENCE. Sound needs silence for it to be distinguishable. Even if you are surrounded by loud noise, there is silence so you can hear it, and that silence is permanent compared to the sounds coming and going.

Content	Context
Stuff	Space
Sounds	Silence

Furthermore, the content of your current experience also includes MOVEMENT. The movement of your chest as you breathe, the movement of your fingers as you progress through this book, the movement of the trees outside your window as the breeze continues to blow. Yet, again, the content of that movement happens within a context of absolute STILLNESS, a stillness that is unaffected by any movement, ever.

Content	Context
Stuff	Space
Sounds	Silence
Movement	Stillness

So we've discovered something quite remarkable during the last few paragraphs – your life, including all of the stuff, sounds and movement, all happens within a context of still silent space. Not only that, but the content comes and goes and is changing, whereas the context is constant and does not change. Incidentally the same is true within your mind; the movements of your thoughts and emotions all occur within a constant context of still silent spaciousness.

Now the million-dollar question:

Where do you tend to focus most of your attention throughout your day — on the content or the context?

Almost everyone, when asked this enlightening question, sees clearly they have been putting most of their attention, most of the time, on the content of their mind and lives. Which is understandable, as this is what we are mainly taught to do when growing up. However, if you want to wake up to a more serene and successful way of working and living, it is paramount to prioritize being attentive to the context. (See page 155 for a fantastic Mind Calm Game for rediscovering the context called 'Noticing Now Space'.)

YOU FEEL WHAT YOU FOCUS ON

There is nothing esoteric or fanciful about this. In a very real way, you feel what you focus on. Putting all of your attention on the things that are moving and changing means you will most likely experience a sense of instability and unease. Also, if you rely on these transient things as your source of success and happiness, it can be a risky strategy. You may well get possessions and prestige, as previously mentioned, but it will rarely relieve the inner itch that there must be more to life than the stuff that's filling your mind and life. You'd be right, too; there is more to life – infinitely more! So, if you want to enjoy a more sustainable sense of success, you can experience it by learning to put your attention on your inner context of life that is permanently still, silent and always abundant.

Shifting where you put your attention — from the content to the context — immediately reconnects you with calm, contentment, love and happiness, and, as a result, true success.

DIVING DEEPER INTO THE CONTENT-CONTEXT

Let's continue our exploration of this model by diving further into the context of... everything! So far we have discovered that content – stuff, sound and movement –

exists within a context of still, silence space. And by putting your attention on the context you can discover an inner calm that is always present. But the benefit of exploring the context of life doesn't end there. In fact it is only the beginning! I started Chapter 1 by asking how you know you have a mind. The answer: *Because you are aware of it.* So, by that rationale, the mind is the content and the context of the mind is your conscious awareness.

Content	Context
Stuff	Space
Sounds	Silence
Movement	Stillness
Mind	Conscious awareness

Without awareness there would be nothing to be aware of the mind. Or, said differently, you would have no way of knowing what your thoughts were if it wasn't for the conscious awareness that was aware of them. An obvious thing to say perhaps, but it is fundamental when learning how to experience mind calm.

> *Have you ever noticed that you still exist even when you are not having any thoughts?*

One of the fun findings of playing with seeing the mind, instead of being the mind, is that thoughts come and go. Not only that but, more importantly, if you are super-alert you will notice how there is a still silent space between your thoughts and an inner spaciousness in which your thoughts take place. What is that still silent space? What continues to exist even when no thoughts are happening?

Yes, you're right: conscious awareness. This means if you want to take on board and apply what this book is all about then you need to rediscover the context of the mind.

WHERE DOES 'NOW' EXIST?

Moving on from the mind, let's take a moment to consider a question relating to time, namely: Where does time actually exist? To answer this, I invite you to consider how you access the past and future. Think back to when you were reading earlier in the chapter. Where does that moment exist now? It is in your mind, right? How about the moment in time when you will eventually finish reading this book? To go to that future moment, you can only go via your mind, using your imagination. This must mean that time exists in the mind. Now I agree there is clearly transition of days and nights – of physical ageing and of dates in your diary – however, any time other than right now can only be accessed via the mind and imagination.

This can be a very exciting discovery if something 'bad' has happened in your past or if you're worrying about the future. It means that if it is not happening right now, then to feel bad about it you've had to go into the past or future by thinking about it in your mind. So learning to stay attentive to the context of this moment means you can let go of the past and future, and enjoy the serenity of this second. Furthermore, it explains why trying to think yourself present won't ever work. If you want to learn how to be in the moment, you can do so by cultivating the habit of being aware of the still silent spacious context, a practice that I like to call 'context awareness'.

Content	Context
Stuff	Space
Sounds	Silence
Movement	Stillness
Mind	Conscious awareness
Time	Present moment

Aware of the context, you naturally become present, as your consciousness is only ever aware of now occurring. Like a silent video camera running in the background, your awareness can only ever be aware of what's happening this moment. Even if you are not aware of your awareness, owing to being distracted by thoughts relating to the past and future, your awareness remains permanently aware of now – only and always; a still watcher seeing from behind your eyes and a silent listener hearing from within your ears.

Even more exciting, being consciously aware, you naturally experience the traits of your awareness and, given the still silent spacious nature of awareness, you start to experience exactly that. You experience more calmness, peace, quietness, expansiveness and much more.

Without knowing the context of still silent spacious consciousness, it is near impossible to be present, feel fulfilled or love unconditionally.

THE NEGATIVE SIDE EFFECTS OF LIVING IN THE CONTENT SIDE OF LIFE

When the mind and time get together they can have a dramatic effect on your sense of success. As we explored in the Judgement Game (see page 4), the mind uses the past and future to compare and contrast how it was and how things could be better in the future. When it does so, we can find things that are wrong.

Judging life negatively often leads to an 'inner no' mind-set towards life, rather than an 'inner yes'. The inner no creates conflict between your inner and outer life experience that is detrimental to your peace and prosperity. It creates an inner sense of angst and inhibits creativity, by making you more prone to living and operating using the fight-or-flight survival areas of your brain. Life in this state becomes very black and white, and much energy and effort is often used to force life to look how you think it should.

Unfortunately the negative knock-on effects of the Judgement Game don't end there. Saying 'no' to life events also often compels you to resist what's happened, is happening or might happen. As you've learned, this inner resistance to life not only puts unhealthy stress upon your body, but is also the hidden cause of fear, frustration, discontentment and a host of other 'negative' emotions.

Content	Context
Stuff	Space
Sounds	Silence
Movement	Stillness
Mind	Conscious awareness
Time	Present moment
Judgement	Is'ness (Love)
Problems	Perfection
Inner no	Inner yes
Resistance	Bring it on
☹ Emotions	☺ Emotions

A SUCCESSFUL LIFE IS ONE THAT YOU LOVE

Now for some very good news! Something very magical happens when you are courageous enough to withdraw your attention from judgemental thinking by placing it on the inner context of stillness. Life stops being good or bad, right or wrong or better or worse, and you see that everything just is. Yes, on the surface things may appear to be bad, wrong or worse, at times, but there is simultaneously what can be described as a mysterious is'ness to life.

Still silent spacious awareness is always perfect, whole and complete exactly as it is. It is beyond judgement because it is beyond the mind. Amazingly, when you suspend judgement, you naturally experience love. Why? With no negative judgement there is no reason not to love.

Successful living on the context side of this model therefore looks and feels very different to the traditional ideas about success taught in school and by society. I'd say a successful life is one that is loved by the person living it. Would you agree? If you met a millionaire who was still unsatisfied with their life or a less wealthy person who loved their life, who would you say is more successful? If you shift your priorities from wanting more stuff to loving what you have, you can very quickly move into a truly successful life – one that you love.

In my experience, the more I am inwardly attentive to the context, the more I experience an inner love of life – irrespective of whether or not my mind judges life as being perfect. In fact, for the record, my mind continues to this day to judge many aspects of my life as not being perfect.

However, despite the opinions of my mind, by choosing to actively place my attention within – on inner still silent space using context awareness – I find that I do what it takes to work with whatever may arise in my life, while simultaneously experiencing the inner love and perfection of the presence residing within conscious awareness.

You don't ignore what's happening in your life. You ignore the judgements your mind has about your life.

Believe it or not, you can enjoy a massive amount of serenity and success by recognizing the is'ness of life. By putting your attention on the context, you rest within an inner yes that allows this moment to be, exactly as it is. The result: peace and a whole host of other 'positive' emotional experiences as well, including joy and love.

INNER STILLNESS = OUTER SUCCESS

How do you know when you are successful? Surely a life lived with an ongoing sense of peace and happiness, love, clarity, creativity and abundance would be one amazingly successful life. Although this book can help you to enjoy more external life success – by accessing more confidence and creativity and getting more done with less stress – this part of the Content–Context model is more about feeling successful on the inside – which, for many, is a major factor in feeling successful.

Content	Context
Failure	Success

Having worked with many highly successful business people at my clinics and retreats, I have observed that true success is not an external thing. Many of the millionaires I've worked with have accomplished more in life and business than most people could dream of. Yet, despite the external success, they don't necessarily feel successful yet.

One of the main reasons for this highly confusing predicament is that, despite their riches, they don't feel successful on the inside, as their focus is entirely on the limited content of their life.

No external possession or position in society can fulfil you if you are missing a huge aspect of your real Self and reality. It costs nothing to rest within the fullness of the context of life. By shifting your attention to the context, you immediately engage with a sense of abundance, completeness and success that is free to everyone; it doesn't require you to prove your worth and has nothing to do with your qualifications, skills or job title.

YOU CAN BE STILL AND STILL GET LOTS DONE!

Being still doesn't mean you become idle; quite the opposite in fact. When you are inwardly aware of stillness, your mind quietens and you naturally experience clarity, intuition and creativity. You enter a heightened state of being that many sportspeople or artists know very well as 'the zone' or 'flow', in which you are present and your thinking mind is out of the way.

From the here and now and with a clear mind, you will be amazed at what can be accomplished. Personally, I rest in this still silent state when writing my books, working with clients at my clinics, running residential retreats, teaching my Academy courses and socializing with friends – as life is so much more effective and enjoyable when I do so. In fact, at school I was told I had dyslexia, so the thought of writing a book still frightens my mind. But, by being still through attentiveness to the context of life, I find the words flow and the fear goes.

Success becomes easier when you are still. By still I don't mean physically sitting or standing still. I'm referring to being attentive to the presence of still silent space within your conscious awareness. From this inner state of being you find that you can remain calm, even when you're faced with a big workload.

When fully present you give your full attention to whatever it is you are doing right now and, given the now is immediate, there is always very little you can do right now. For example, writing a book is a daunting and potentially stressful task, but writing this word is very easy and takes very little effort. By remaining present while progressing through whatever work requires your attention, you deal with what's in front of you now, and then move on to the next thing and then the next. Before you know it you've written a book, built a business or achieved something pretty spectacular – all with very little stress and while enjoying a great deal of serenity. You get to enjoy the journey properly and experience the destination as a bonus, not a necessity.

FROM FRUSTRATION TO FREEDOM

Until a person develops the skill of context awareness by being consciously aware, they can suffer from what can best be described as a hellish life! In other words, they spend their days missing life, distracted by incessant judgemental thinking about the past and future. Their enjoyment of life goes up and down, depending on which side of the Judgement Game they happen to end up on. If they end up on the negative, bad, worse or wrong side then life can end up feeling like a never-ending series of problems needing to be fixed or avoided. They never quite get 'there'.

When things don't go to plan they often end up resisting life, which leads to unnecessary stress and heartache. Not to mention a sense of being a failure, irrespective of what they achieve, as their mind convinces them that they are never quite 'there' yet. In order to make things better and get 'there', people lost in the content side of life often end up being overly controlling, manipulating and managing life in a bid to make things better, which all contributes to prolonging the frustrating and unfortunate cycle.

Thankfully, on the other side, freedom is waiting for anyone willing to search out a new way of relating to life. The more you can learn to let life be, by resting in the calm that resides within the context, the less you need to control what happens. It becomes clear that the opposite of control is freedom. By that I mean that the less you need to control life, the freer you become. And the freer you are, the more serene and successful you naturally and automatically feel.

Given the choice I don't know anyone who would choose hell over heaven. If you take a step back and look at the two lists on the next page, I hope it is much clearer that being lost in the content is very unappealing when compared to resting in the context of conscious awareness. This alone is a great motivation to meditate! When you come back to the context you become present and experience the perfection of is'ness, and the serenity that comes from disengaging negative thinking and instead having an inner 'yes' to life.

Content	Context
Stuff	Space
Sounds	Silence
Movement	Stillness
Mind	Conscious awareness
Time	Present moment
Judgement	Is'ness (love)
Problems	Perfection
Inner no	Inner yes
Resistance	Bring it on
☹ Emotions	☺ Emotions
Failure	Success
Control	Freedom
CHAOTIC MIND	MIND CALM

Moving your attention from the content to the context is one of the most important skills you can develop. It frees you from problem-based thinking for good, and gives you the living experience of nirvana now. So how can you make the shift? One of the most powerful ways to cultivate the habit of context awareness is, of course, meditation. And the best news of all is that the wait is over. Next up, I will teach you Mind Calm meditation.

Chapter 7

MIND CALM MEDITATION TECHNIQUE

The purpose of meditation is to be your Self: to rest into your conscious awareness. Remember your consciousness is already perfectly well, calm and content; it is your permanent most powerful Self. It is the underlying still silent spacious foundational context in which all physical, emotional and life movement happens. Consciousness is the being in which all doing occurs. A natural consequence of reconnecting with your being once again is that you need to be willing to let go of doing, trying and exerting effort when meditating. Such a turnaround in how you engage life requires a very simple way to meditate such as Mind Calm, which reveals the exquisite quiet presence of your being within.

In this chapter I'll share the three steps required for Mind Calm meditation. Before I do, however, I want to make it very clear that you should engage with the 'steps' in the most effortless way possible, without any 'doing' on your part. To engage in any effort when meditating actually moves you away from your natural state of being. You'll discover that 'you are the real you' when you are not trying to be someone or something else.

> *You do not make yourself calm. On the contrary, calm will happen to you when you stop trying to be calm!*

Trying to get these steps right can actually be counterproductive, frustrating and, in the main, ineffective. Instead, they are given more as awareness-raising guidelines, which will quickly and effortlessly move you into an aware state of conscious being. The steps shared are to be used as a way of highlighting when you've left the present moment, started thinking and stopped being consciously aware. So, to get the most from Mind Calm, make it your intention not to try to find or force calm. Instead let calm occur by letting go of doing anything except being attentive to whatever naturally presents itself each moment you meditate.

Consider this: What remains present within you when you let go of your thoughts, emotions, physical sensations and stories in your head about your life?

> *By letting go of what you are not you will find the magnificent being that you have been the entire time.*

Whenever you're using Mind Calm, aim to notice when you are thinking and be willing to let the thoughts go so that you can return to present moment awareness. I appreciate the thoughts can be personal and about things

TOP TIP: LET GO OF EVERYTHING THAT CAN BE LET GO

When I first learned to meditate, my meditation teachers told me about this amazing thing called 'still silence'. Naturally, in my desire to experience the same peace and joy as the teachers, I started looking for the 'still silence' that they spoke of so splendidly. It was only after many months of frustrated meditations that I finally realized that the act of trying to find the 'still silence' was the very thing moving me away from it! The more I looked for it, the more I missed it. It was almost as if I was looking away from my Self in an attempt to find myself. So please hear me when I say, don't try to find 'conscious awareness' or be calm. You become consciously aware when you engage GAAWO, which in turn will reveal still silence. Relax and let it happen. If anything be more interested in noticing what remains when you let go of everything that can be let go of – because if you can let it go it then it's not permanent and therefore not you.

that are important to you; however, thinking all the time hasn't brought you the peace, love and joy that your heart yearns for – so let the thoughts go. Similarly, I want you to notice when you are engaged in an emotion – positive or negative – and let it go too, to return to present moment awareness. And I want you to notice when you have become distracted by body sensations and return to present moment awareness. Quite simply I invite you to notice when you are busy doing instead of effortlessly consciously being.

CALM = CONSCIOUS AWARENESS LIFE MEDITATION

Seeing the subtle movement away from present moment awareness to engage in the content of your mind and being willing to let go to return to the context of consciousness awareness is the primary purpose of this beautifully simple form of meditation. The 'CALM' part of MIND CALM is an acronym that stands for 'Conscious Awareness Life Meditation'. Mind Calm is therefore quite simply a form of meditation that makes you consciously aware during everyday life. We've already covered the many beneficial reasons for being consciously aware, so let's turn our attention now to what the meditation includes and how to do it.

Mind Calm involves two main elements:

1.   Being Gently Alert with your Attention Wide Open (GAAWO), and

2.   Occasionally thinking Calm Thoughts that help to bring more of what you want into daily life.

An earlier chapter introduced you to GAAWO (see page 44), when you learned how to be gently alert with your attention wide open with your eyes open. Now you are ready to play with GAAWO with your eyes closed. To do this, I want you to start with open-eyed GAAWO by looking ahead at the page while letting your attention open up wide. Now, having engaged GAAWO with your eyes open, I invite you to see what it is like to let your eyelids drop down, while keeping GAAWO gently engaged. Do it now and see what it is like. You may find that the experience between open- and closed-eye GAAWO is very similar. Yes, you might not have external objects to notice in your peripheral vision.

But nonetheless, by having the intention to be gently alert with your attention wide open with your eyes closed, you will find that your mind is more still and quiet.

Every Calm Sitting – which is the term we use for the more traditional closed-eye sitting meditation – starts with closing your eyes and engaging GAAWO. You are encouraged to 'hang out' in GAAWO for a while, to practise being consciously aware and become more intimate with the calm context of this moment. Then, after a little while (I'm not going to tell you how long because you might start timing it), gently think a Calm Thought.

THE 10 CALM THOUGHTS

Calm Thoughts are ones that you are given to intentionally think during open- and closed-eye Mind Calm meditation. They can help you to bring very appealing states of being into your conscious living experience, such as peace, love and clarity, to name only three of the 10 states covered in Mind Calm (see page 90 for the full series of Calm Thoughts.) Even if you might not believe it yet, you are already connected, powerful, joyful, peace-filled, love and one with everything in the cosmos. You are all of these stunning states of being and more. However, if you haven't been experiencing them then it means they've become buried under your busy mind. These states are like seeds in the soil and using the Calm Thoughts gives them a chance to break through the surface to become visible once again.

Calm Thoughts are unique and bring these states of being into your conscious living experience because of the following three components that make them up:

OM + Positive Intention + Focus Point

Component 1: OM

'OM' (sometimes spelled 'AUM') is a well-known and widely used word from Sanskrit, an ancient language of consciousness. One of the facets of Sanskrit that makes it so conscious is that it is a vibrational language. This means Sanskrit shares the vibrational experience of the meaning of the words you are thinking or speaking. Quite remarkably, when using Sanskrit you automatically align your attention with the vibrational frequency of the words you are thinking or saying. This can be very powerful. Especially when you appreciate just how much of the universe is impacted by and connected via vibration.

> *'Everything in life is vibration.'*
> ALBERT EINSTEIN

Modern science has found what the ancient mystics knew all along: everything in the physical world is vibrating at a range of frequencies that enables them to maintain their individual physical forms. Quantum physicists have said that when you delve down to the subatomic particle level and beyond to even tinier levels, all you find is light potentials coming in and out of existence. Wow! At the quantum level, everything is vibrating at frequencies, which, as you return to viewing them with the naked eye, end up being a tree, a chair, a pen or the book in your hands.

At the subatomic level, which is beyond what can be seen, heard or touched by your senses, even your body is vibrating at a range of frequencies that ends up being your skin, muscles, bones, brain and all of the organs that are doing their magic right now. But what makes this even more miraculous is how beyond the blatant components of your physical body, your thoughts and emotions are also vibrating and creating a ripple effect throughout not only your body but the entire universe, too. Wow, again! Sounds cool, but what does all of this have to do with OM?

At the base level of everything in physical, mental and emotional existence is one root vibration. You will never guess what that vibration is... Yes, you guessed right, OM! Although more recently, scientists have referred to this root vibration in terms such as 'the tone of the known universe', the ancient mystical traditions know this to be the OM.

OM is known as being the vibration of creation: the father and mother vibration present at the birth of everything in existence.

I like to think about it this way. Imagine that in the beginning – and I mean the 'big beginning' where nothing existed yet – there was only still silent empty space. Then movement came from the stillness, sound from the silence and stuff started to fill the empty space. The first movement vibration from stillness was OM, the first vibration that produced sound was OM, and the first vibration that ended up as something physical was OM. Fast forward to the present day and this means that OM is the root vibration of everything in your life, including your thoughts, emotions and physical body, along with everybody you know and everything that has happened, is happening and will happen in your life. Everything comes into creation on the coat-tails of OM.

Putting your attention on OM, especially when meditating, aligns your attention with the driving force of creation.

Pretty cool, hey! I guess this is one of the reasons why millions of people have meditated using OM for as long as people have meditated. But the good news doesn't end here. Remember, quantum scientists have found everything comes in and out of existence each moment. This phenomenon leads us to the liberating possibility that 'in the beginning' is eternally now.

> *Every moment offers a fresh start full of potential for you to bring into creation what you want — if you invite it in.*

Being stuck in the same thinking patterns you had yesterday, last week and the previous decades, invites the same old stuff to keep coming into existence time and time again. But what if you had a brand new thought; one carried on the infinitely powerful wings of OM – to help you bring new life into your life? Well, this is what the Calm Thoughts offer because we marry OM with positive intentions.

Component 2: Positive intentions

Thoughts become things. If you've ever read a self-help book, or observed how your life works, there's a high chance you'll already know that everything you have purposefully created during your life started out as a single seed-thought. For instance, you once thought, *I'd like to get a job* or *start a business* and like magic – OK, potentially with a lot of work too – your intention to make a change in your career came into fruition. Or, perhaps, you thought you'd really like more mind calm and *BAM*, this book ended up in your hands. It is happening all of the time. Thoughts make the journey from inside your mind to transform into external physical events and things. Take a look at your life today and you will see the reflection of the ripple effect of what you've been thinking about most over the past few days, weeks or years. The evidence is in plain sight: thoughts become things eventually.

> *Thought-based positive intentions are*
> *seeds of potential.*

Rolling around in your mind playing the Judgement Game and putting your attention on what's bad, negative, wrong or worse leads to the re-creation of what you don't want. Good things may happen occasionally, (what goes down does go up, after all), but for those lost in judgemental thinking, life can become a struggle up and over a never-ending hill of hurdles. To bring an end to the unnecessary cycle, Mind Calm includes a series of ten positive intentions to focus your attention upon instead.

But with Mind Calm you don't just try to think positively from the surface level of your mind. Instead, you start Mind Calm by engaging GAAWO to align your attention with present moment awareness then think OM (the driving force of creation) alongside the positive intentions. As you can imagine, this ends up being a potent combo bringing about big positive effects. Especially when you add the final component of the Calm Thoughts, which helps you to cross the bridge from the mind into your conscious living experience.

Component 3: Focus points

Each Calm Thought has a recommended location within or around your body on which to put your attention when thinking it. With the addition of these focus points, the power of the Calm Thoughts is magnified significantly.

Focus points work in a number of ways. First, a few of the focus point locations sit within some of the well-known energy centres in your body called chakras. Known for centuries and taught in many traditions, chakra is a Sanskrit word translated as 'wheel' or 'vortex'. By placing your attention on these areas of your body while thinking the Calm Thoughts, you not only activate the energy vortexes more but also harness their power to actualize the positive intentions.

Those familiar with chakras may notice that some of the positive intentions and focus points don't link up with the traditional meanings or purpose of each chakra. This is intentional, as Mind Calm is a more modern way of meditating, which also aims to harness the power of the symbolic nature of the mind. The mind uses and responds to symbols. Therefore, giving the mind symbolic locations within the body to focus on makes the mind less likely to judge and resist the process.

For example, most people feel their emotions in their solar plexus area (which is located between the navel and the heart). So to think *OM PEACE* while focusing on the solar plexus – which is actually one of the Calm Thoughts – makes sense to your mind as that is the body area where most people would prefer to experience peace. By working in harmony with the symbolic nature of the mind, you can more easily create mind calm and, without such a busy mind, rediscover the still silent presence of your conscious awareness. But what about the other focus points, which don't sit within the known chakras? The same goes for these too. You will notice that these focus points are also in areas within or around your body that symbolically relate to the positive intention that the Calm Thought represents.

Despite this reasoning behind each Calm Thought, I encourage you not to get too caught up in the individual themes or theory behind how they might work. The most important part of Mind Calm is the way in which you use them. Before taking you through Mind Calm meditation in detail, here's a quick summary, so you can quickly see how simple and easy this form of meditation is...

MIND CALM MEDITATION – AT A GLANCE

Step 1: GAAWO
Be Gently Alert with your Attention Wide Open.

Step 2: Calm Thought
Think one of the Calm Thoughts (see page 90).

Step 3: GAAWO
Be Gently Alert with your Attention Wide Open.

When you notice you've been thinking, repeat cycle.

Always begin using Mind Calm by engaging GAAWO. Then once you are gently alert with your attention wide open, think one of the Calm Thoughts. As soon as you have thought the Calm Thought, let go the thought and focus point by returning to GAAWO. Rest in calm conscious awareness until you notice that you've been thinking about something, then repeat the three Steps. Simple! Believe me – Mind Calm is profound and powerful in its simplicity and conscious raising benefits.

THE 10 CALM THOUGHTS

There are 10 Calm Thoughts in total, each consisting of 'OM', a positive intention and a focus point.

OM + Intentions		Focus point
OM Presence	10	In Entire Body
OM Oneness	9	Far and Wide
OM Wisdom	8	Top of Head
OM Clarity	7	Forehead Centre
OM Truth	6	Throat
OM Love	5	Heart Centre
OM Peace	4	Solar Plexus
OM Joy	3	Navel
OM Power	2	Base of Spine
OM Connection	1	Soles of Feet

MIND CALM SITTING USING ALL 10 CALM THOUGHTS

Now you are aware of the three steps involved in Mind Calm and are aware of the 10 Calm Thoughts, let's go through a Calm Sitting together.

- Begin by sitting comfortably, close your eyes, and engage GAAWO by being gently alert with your attention wide open.

- Think OM CONNECTION with your attention on the soles of your feet... Let go of the thought and focus point by re-engaging GAAWO. Rest consciously aware of now until you notice you've been thinking other thoughts.

- Then engage GAAWO for a short while before thinking OM POWER with your attention at the base of your spine... Let go of the thought and focus point by re-engaging GAAWO. Rest consciously aware of now until you notice you've been thinking other thoughts.

- Then engage GAAWO for a short while before thinking OM JOY with your attention in the navel. Then let go of the thought and focus point by re-engaging GAAWO. Rest consciously aware of now until you notice you've been thinking other thoughts.

- Then engage GAAWO for a short while before thinking OM PEACE with your attention in your solar plexus... then let go of the thought and focus point by re-engaging GAAWO. Rest consciously aware of now until you notice you've been thinking other thoughts.

- Then engage GAAWO for a short while before thinking OM LOVE with your attention in your heart centre... Let go of the thought and focus point by re-engaging GAAWO. Rest consciously aware of now until you notice you've been thinking other thoughts.

- Then engage GAAWO for a short while before thinking OM TRUTH with your attention in your throat area... Let go of the thought and focus point by re-engaging GAAWO. Rest consciously aware of now until you notice you've been thinking other thoughts.

- Then engage GAAWO for a short while before thinking OM CLARITY with your attention in the centre of your forehead... Let go of the thought and focus point by re-engaging GAAWO. Rest consciously aware of now until you notice you've been thinking other thoughts.

- Then engage GAAWO for a short while before thinking OM WISDOM with your attention at the top of your head... Let go of the thought and focus point by re-engaging GAAWO. Rest consciously aware of now until you notice you've been thinking other thoughts.

- Then engage GAAWO for a short while before thinking OM ONENESS with your attention far and wide... Let go of the thought and focus point by re-engaging GAAWO. Rest consciously aware of now until you notice you've been thinking other thoughts.

- Then engage GAAWO for a short while before thinking OM PRESENCE with your attention in the entire body... Let go of the thought and focus point by re-engaging GAAWO. Rest consciously aware of now until you notice you've been thinking other thoughts.

- Either repeat the series of Calm Thoughts or if you're ready to finish the Calm Sitting, slowly open your eyes.

TOP TIP: GAAWO ON THE GO

Mind Calm is not only for when you close your eyes a couple of times a day, but for being consciously aware throughout daily life. It is great, when you finish your Calm Sitting, to immediately engage GAAWO with your eyes open as you begin to get on with your day. This can help to make present moment awareness a habit that is effortless and natural.

ADDITIONAL OPTIONS FOR A CALM SITTING

One of the great things about Mind Calm is that there are not actually any fixed rules to abide by. On the contrary, Mind Calm offers a range of different ways that you can use it to suit your individual preferences and ever-changing requirements.

Although we have gone through a more traditional Calm Sitting, whereby you use all of the Calm Thoughts in the order they've been listed on page 90, you are free to use them in whatever way works best for you. The most common three Calm Sitting options are listed below.

1. Use every Calm Thought

Follow similar instructions to the ones outlined on page 91. Set the intention at the beginning of your Calm Sitting to use all ten of your Calm Thoughts. Then close your eyes, engage GAAWO and go! You might think each Calm Thought only once before moving on to the next (good if you don't have much time) or if you want to play more or have a busy mind that day, you might end up using each Calm Thought a few times each before moving on to the next.

2. Use only one Calm Thought

Start by considering what you would like to focus on most during the Calm Sitting. Perhaps you want more peace, or maybe you feel you could benefit from being more loving. Or possibly you have noticed that you are lacking clarity so decide to focus on that. When you know which Calm Thought you want to use, close your eyes, engage GAAWO and get going with your focused Calm Sitting.

3. Use the Calm Thoughts you tend to avoid

Begin by considering which of the 10 Calm Thoughts you tend to feel uncomfortable using, or tend to avoid altogether. Any avoidance or discomfort when using specific Calm Thoughts can mean there is a block or resistance and you could benefit from healing your relationship with it. By giving them your time, attention and love you will find that any blocks to using the Calm Thoughts fade away and you may also notice improvements in that area of your life.

CALM MOMENTS: OPEN-EYED PRACTICE

Speed up the cultivation of your habit of being inwardly attentive to stillness by using Mind Calm meditation with your eyes open through what I like to call 'Calm Moments'. For such moments, choose one of the Calm Thoughts and set the intention at the beginning of the day to think it whenever you remember throughout your day. Then, whenever you remember to do so, engage eyes-open GAAWO, think your Calm Thought and move on with your day until the next time you remember and do it again. By having open-eyed Calm Moments during daily life you can find your results are magnified exponentially.

RECOMMENDED DAILY PRACTICE

Thinking too much, getting stressed and missing the present moment during the rush of modern life is a habit. Thankfully, so is enjoying peace with your mind. Mind Calm helps you to make the inner shift from having all of your attention on the content of your life (your ever-changing thoughts, emotions, body and life circumstances) to redirecting your focus to the present moment peace-filled context of life. For the best results I recommend you do two or three Mind Calm sittings every day, each lasting between 10 and 20 minutes. Good times of the day are when you first wake up in the morning, mid-afternoon, before your evening meal and as you go to sleep at night.

Little and often is the best way to optimize the results from Mind Calm, which is great news because everyone has 10–20 minutes to spare here and there throughout their day. On top of your closed-eye Calm Sittings, have regular Calm Moments with your eyes open throughout your day whenever you remember. For Calm Moments, simply engage eyes-open GAAWO, think a Calm Thought and continue with whatever you are doing, until the next time you remember.

For the most transformative beginning to your Mind Calm practice, do the 10-part Mind Calm Programme shared in Part II (see page 137) of this book.

MOTIVATION TO MEDITATE

You now know a meditation technique and have been given a number of different ways to bring it into your day. However, let's be honest, meditation only works if you do it. I'm very aware that you might already have a busy life and I'm suggesting you add something new to your perhaps already full schedule. So to encourage you to commit to a regular Mind Calm routine, this is a good time to remind yourself of your heart's highest hope, which you clarified in Chapter 3 (see page 37). Not only will this help you to get going, but it can also keep you going during times when you experience the diverse range of happenings that can occur when meditating.

Chapter 8

INTRIGUING MEDITATION HAPPENINGS

Intriguing things happen when sitting still during meditation, which makes this chapter perhaps one of the most important in the book. Although a lot of the time you are likely to enjoy Mind Calm, there are some things that may happen that it's worth knowing about in advance. If you are not aware of what might happen when meditating, and why, then there's a very big chance that you will think you're doing it wrong, it's not working and, most tragic of all, quit before enjoying the big benefits possible.

> *Knowing the common meditation*
> *happenings helps you to continue with*
> *confidence that Mind Calm is working.*

Proceeding unaware of these meditation happenings, there's also a high chance you might become frustrated and resist what happens. Such an attitude makes meditations unnecessarily uncomfortable. So please take heed of what I'm about to share – it can be the difference between Mind Calm being the meditation technique that you've been looking for versus feeling let down by a practice that offered so much but failed to deliver the results you thought you wanted.

THE THEORY BEHIND THE ACTIVITY

Earlier in the book I mentioned that it is the mind's natural tendency to want to be happy. When it comes to your body, it has the natural predisposition to heal anytime it is given the opportunity. Mind Calm offers it this chance. When you close your eyes, engage GAAWO and start playing with your Calm Thoughts, you will find that your body gets to enjoy a great deal of rest.

When the body rests it heals.

Healing is an active process: stored stresses from the past day, week, year or decade are released by the body while maintenance and repair projects are also undertaken by your incredible inner intelligence. Due to the scientifically proven mind–body connection, all of this very natural and positive healing activity in your body is reflected in your mind – with things moving in there, too.

During your lifetime your body has picked up stress. You may have had a difficult childhood, experienced some trauma, gone through difficult relationship splits, and/or simply dealt with a range of pressures relating to your family, finances, work, home and so on. For some people, there simply aren't enough hours in the night to get enough sleep to release all of the stresses that have been gathered over the previous day, week, years or decades. So when you sit down to meditate, it is very common for the body to immediately want to set about releasing the accumulated stress. This movement in your body can be witnessed within the mind in a number of different ways, with the top eight common meditation happenings shared now.

EIGHT COMMON MEDITATION HAPPENINGS TO WATCH OUT FOR...

Happening 1: Memories

While your mind does its best to make sense of stress-releasing activity occurring in the body, you may notice memories crop up. These could be memories from what happened earlier that day or relate to events that happened much earlier in your life. If they are 'positive', you can end up falling into a mind trap of giving them too much attention. If you do, you will leave the present moment, no longer be consciously aware and end up lost in reminiscent thinking. Albeit nice for a while, positive memories are dead when compared to the awe-inspiring aliveness of the here and now – so let them go.

At the other end of the memory spectrum are those you'd rather forget for good. Whenever negative memories come to mind it is common to want to drop into analysing them or feel compelled to push them away: *Why am I remembering this old memory? I thought I'd dealt with that memory in therapy years ago. I guess that was another waste of money then!* No, not at all, as I'm sure the therapy did provide benefit. However, what you are witnessing during your Mind Calm sitting is your body finally getting around to releasing it. This is a very positive thing! You want to let the memory pass freely through your awareness and let it go. Remember, you become attached to what you resist. Pushing negative memories away gives them unwarranted power and is counterproductive, as resistance causes more stress. The best thing to do whenever you notice negative memories in your mind is to engage GAAWO. Yes, your mind might immediately want to grab your attention back again by recalling the memory. If that happens, be courageous by rising above judging and resisting the memory thought by again letting it go with the help of GAAWO. After a while, you will find the memory fades away as you stop giving any of your attention to it.

TOP TIP: PEACE WITH MIND PROTOCOL

For more stubborn negative memories, which you find yourself compelled to think at length about, check out the Peace with Mind Protocol (see page 121) for a highly effective non-therapeutic way to get peace with the more intense memories that don't want to budge.

Happening 2: Abstract dreams

Multiple stresses being released simultaneously from your body can show up in your mind as abstract dream-like images. Dreams are one of the ways your mind makes sense of a group of stresses releasing at the same time, which helps to explain why you tend to dream most at night when your body reaches its deepest levels of rest.

Although it is common to want to analyse your dreams, perhaps with the positive intention of finding out what they can teach you, this can also be a mind trap.

Dream interpretation justifies lots of thinking and again acts as a distraction from present moment awareness. Despite some dreams being fascinating, not to mention funny, let them go as fast as they appear by returning to GAAWO and continuing with your Calm Sitting. Doing so will allow the body to heal more quickly and lead to more Mind Calm in the long run.

Happening 3: Millions of thoughts

Every so often you will have an absolutely amazing meditation when your body releases a huge amount of stress and undertakes multiple healing and repair projects simultaneously. The only problem with these meditations is that you might not feel that they are amazing – mainly because all the healing activity in your body can appear in your mind as millions of thoughts!

During busy Calm Sittings like these, it is common for the commentator in your mind to pipe up unhelpfully: *This isn't working* or *I think I will stop for now and try again later*. If you aren't careful you can let your mind stop you from benefiting from a highly healing meditation. It is vitally important to be clear that Mind Calm is about enjoying peace of mind sometimes and peace with mind the rest of the time. Busy Calm Sittings are great opportunities for you to practise being at peace with your thoughts. Let them come and go, while remembering they do so within the context of calm conscious awareness. If you try to avoid busy Calm

Sittings or resist them when they happen, then you will never enjoy the inner freedom and fearlessness that peace with mind provides.

> *The sky doesn't care how many birds are flying through it or if they are black birds or white turtledoves. Similarly, conscious awareness does not care about the quality or quantity of thoughts happening within it.*

Only your mind cares about how many thoughts happen or whether they are pretty thoughts or ugly. Whenever you are having what feel like millions of thoughts, then engage GAAWO and play with seeing the thoughts instead of being the thoughts.

Upon noticing lots of thoughts happening, it is common for the mind to produce thoughts about the thoughts. In cases like these, you are essentially having thoughts about thoughts, which is quite funny if you think about it! Your mind will want to judge the amount or content of the thoughts happening. If you don't see the judgement thoughts about your thoughts then you will suffer from resisting their existence and risk ending your Calm Sitting prematurely. Trust me, thinking about thinking is perhaps one of the most pointless kinds of thinking, so remember:

> *Lots of thoughts when meditating equals lots of healing!*

TOP TIP: TRUST YOUR MIRRORS

Do you want to know one of the funniest things about meditation and the mind? The purpose of meditating regularly is not to change your mind but, instead, to rest in conscious awareness and thus change your relationship with your mind. This means that if you leave present moment awareness to check in with the mind to ask it how you're getting on, it will more often than not say that nothing has changed. And it could be right. Nothing might have changed when it comes to the content of the mind. The same old thought patterns may continue. However, despite this, if you ask the people in your life how you're getting on, they will often tell you that you are consistently more calm, kinder and happier.

Thanks to the Judgement Game, the Resist Persist, the Attach Catch and the Time Trap, your mind might never be truly calm, contented or happy. Thankfully you don't have to wait. Engage GAAWO and make it your priority to be aware of the inner consciousness that has no reason not to be happy, peaceful, loving and free.

Meditation works if you do it often enough. Keep going even if your mind tells you to stop. Suspend self-judgement by trusting the wise people in your life when they reflect back to you the changes that they see in you.

Happening 4: Emotional energy

Another common meditation happening is emotions. Thoughts and emotions go hand in hand. Either you will have thoughts and a corresponding emotion will occur, or your mind will notice an emotional energy within the body and start thinking about what it is, why you're feeling that way, label it as positive or negative, and start planning how to get rid of it, if judged as bad. Irrespective, it is highly beneficial to treat your emotions in a similar way to your thoughts – see them and let them be present without interfering in the natural mind–body activity.

Peace with emotions

When I first started meditating, I was going through a relationship split: losing a child that I'd been raising because she wasn't biologically 'mine', losing the house that I'd been living in, along with a business that I'd worked very hard to help build, too. In short, I thought I was losing my family, home, career and financial stability, and it was one of the most challenging times in my life.

When I sat down to meditate, do you think there was only calm and stillness? Absolutely not!

All the stress from the break-up and sadness and fear from the imposed life changes had to be released. Experiencing a huge amount of inner turmoil, my mind wanted to think in depth about what was happening and how I could fix it. As a result of all the thinking, I felt flooded with a host of intense emotions, from anger to despair. In an attempt to feel better, I ended up using meditation to try to make the bad feelings go away. However, in doing so, I completely missed the point of meditation, which is largely about learning to be at peace with your thoughts, emotions and life in general.

What I didn't realize at the time was that my attachment to making my negative emotions go away was actually making them stick around longer. Totally unintentionally, by wishing them gone, I was actually focusing my attention on them. I would constantly 'check in' to see if they'd moved on yet, which didn't give them any space to leave or be present within me. In addition, I also didn't see my mind-based judgements and resistance towards the way I was feeling. All in all, it led to a really uncomfortable and frustrating start to my meditation journey.

Since then, I've actively played with befriending my feelings and giving them space to be. By consciously breathing in a balanced and deep way (most people hold their breath if they don't want to feel something) and seeing the judgements in my mind about the emotions, I've found they immediately stop being 'negative'. Instead, they fill my body with life-giving energy and often end up being a delightful part of any meditation sitting.

So if you, too, find yourself experiencing what your mind labels as negative emotions, then see what happens when you engage GAAWO and let them be within you without any resistance.

By being consciously aware and letting the emotions be present within you, you may find that they pass on through or stick around. Either way, you won't care and will enjoy the liberation that comes from having peace with emotions.

Happening 5: Physical sensations

Stress moving around and releasing from the body also shows up in a range of physical sensations. You might get an itch, a temporary twitch, or even a passing pain somewhere in your body. Out of habit it is common for the mind to want to judge and resist any unexpected physical sensations. Again, this can be a mind trap if you intentionally engage in lots of thinking about the sensation: *What is it? Why is it here? How long might it stick around? How can I make it go away?*

Peace with pain

Whenever you notice a painful physical sensation it is very useful to engage GAAWO and temporarily focus on it. To be clear, in circumstances like these with symptoms of physical pain, you should pay attention to the physical sensations, not the thoughts you might be having in your mind about the pain. This distinction is important, as it's the difference between experiencing pain or suffering. Suffering occurs when you start thinking about the physical pain. Get the difference?

I appreciate that there is a fine line between pain and suffering, especially if it is intensely uncomfortable. Your mind might say *I'm suffering due to my intense pain.* However, the reality of the situation is the suffering stems from engaging in judgemental thinking about the pain. By seeing the mind-based judgements and resistance towards the physical sensation, you can peacefully co-exist with physical discomfort. This is genuinely amazing news as it means you don't have to wait until your physical body changes or improves before you can rest into the calming context of conscious awareness.

Let pain or other physical sensations be your teacher, providing immediate feedback as to when you are consciously aware or lost in your thoughts about the stuff happening in your body.

For some people, becoming super aware and watching the sensations causes them to diminish or even disappear. For others they may continue, but the suffering won't. It goes without saying that pain is your body's way of telling you that something needs attention. You might need to seek professional guidance from health practitioners and actively do things to help your body heal. The main thing to know is that all kinds of physical sensations can happen when you meditate and, if they do, let them come and go in the knowledge that you are witnessing stress being released, healing being undertaken and, in some cases, your body speaking the mind.

Happening 6: Sleeps and meeps

If the body–mind needs rest, you may find you fall fast asleep during meditation. This is perfectly natural and shouldn't be resisted. However, if you find yourself falling asleep every time you attempt a Calm Sitting then you might need to make a few minor adjustments to your meditation routine.

Although there are no strict sitting postures, if you're lying flat out on a comfy couch or bed, all snug and warm wrapped in your favourite blanket, then it might not lead to the most alert meditation and sleep might be inevitable! So, if you fall asleep more often than not, it might be useful to sit more upright. The further back your head rests, the less alert you will usually be and the more thoughts will normally happen. So sit up, while always making sure you are comfortable and at ease, as discomfort can act as an unnecessary distraction from the purpose of Mind Calm.

Shortening the length of time of your Calm Sittings can also help. It is better to have 10–20 minutes of alert Mind Calm than a sleepy meander through an hour. Also, you might want to add some variety to when you meditate. I used to meditate every day at 4 p.m. for a couple of hours; however, I found it was the time in the day my body wanted a siesta. So these days I meditate at times of the day when I'm generally more awake.

Monitor your most wakeful times of the day
and close your eyes to maximize
the conscious-raising results.

Exercising before a Calm Sitting can make you more physiologically alert, too. There's no need to run a marathon or anything too strenuous. Two or three yoga postures, a few star jumps or a walk up the stairs will suffice and, when combined with a refreshing drink of good quality water, you'll find that your chances of falling asleep drop. Overall, with sleep, the key is not to resist the natural needs of your body. If you need to sleep you will, but if you sleep every time you meditate, then you won't be having a regular meditation routine, but instead, you're having what I affectionately call a 'meep'. Meeps are sleeps that start off with a short meditation! For the best results, aim to be alert when you meditate – you are closing your eyes in order to wake up, after all.

Happening 7: Peace, love, joy and oneness

Don't worry. It isn't all 'bad' news! Using Mind Calm can also lead to copious amounts of peace, joy and love too. You will enjoy times of feeling an immense deep peace, as if you are resting in a still ocean of calm. Joy can bubble up when learning to let go of the mind. In happy times like these, you will notice a big smile on your face and might even need to laugh out loud. Let the joy flow, as it wants to naturally.

> *Love and oneness can be a very beautiful side effect of letting go of judgement, resistance and attachment, and resting into the presence of your being.*

Mind-based constructs that have created the illusion of a separate 'me' fall away, leaving a love-filled unified consciousness in its place. You feel a great love and compassion towards yourself and everyone you meet. Irrespective of how long you've known them, what their personality happens to be like, or any other criteria your mind may have previously relied on to deem others loveable. As you let go of your mind-based rulebook of requirements of what people, places, events or things must be like for them to be loveable, you naturally fall in love all day long. Naturally, you connect with others from your unconditional heart that only ever wants to give love without needing anything in return. It is my hope that you will experience the love-filled oneness that is the natural by-product of being one with the consciousness that resides within you, everyone else, everything else and the space in between.

TOP TIP: THE MIND CANNOT COPY STILLNESS

The mind is moving, consisting of thoughts and emotions that come and go. Therefore, your mind cannot mimic the experience of still silent space. As a result, you are genuinely beyond your mind when you're in the present moment, directly experiencing consciousness when you are attentive to the presence of still silent space within. Knowing this helps to avoid confusion as to whether or not you are present, allowing you to be confident that if you are ever thinking about whether you are present, you can be sure at that moment you're not!

Happening 8: Still silent space

Stillness, silence and spaciousness can be savoured too. When meditating, if you become aware of a stillness or quietness or bigness, then gently put your attention on these qualities. In times like these you are directly experiencing consciousness. Remember the mind only exists when it's moving. The mind gives the appearance of a voice in your head that can sound loud at times. And the mind, due to its conceptual thought-based nature, can be limiting and constrictive. So being attentive to the still silent space is a very good sign that you are beyond the confines of your mind, resting in the infinite.

A great spiritual teacher once said, 'Be still and know that you are God.' These clear and concise eight words share, perhaps, the only strategy you ultimately need to live a liberated life free from mind-based fear, and full of peace, love and joy. Furthermore, in my humble opinion, I'd suggest knowing you are not separate from divinity, and living each day experiencing the presence of the unbounded within, is a big reason why you were born.

BE STILL AND LET EVERYTHING GO

Stress will want to release, healing will want to take place and the mind will play its games. Just don't buy into the belief that Mind Calm meditation isn't working if you encounter memories, get lost occasionally in dream-like mental concoctions, have millions of thoughts or uneasy emotions, notice physical sensations or sometimes sleep or meep. Inevitably, all these things will happen, sometimes all in the same Calm Sitting! The only part of you that will ever care how your meditation looks and feels is your mind. Be free to simply be – by letting it all go.

There are no 'good' or 'bad' meditations
— it is only judgemental thinking
that makes them appear so.

Stunning states of being, including peace, joy, and love, are waiting to be cherished and enjoyed. All you need to do, to reconnect with the array of beautiful fragrances that make up your being, is be willing to release your grasp on the mind. Turn your attention towards present moment awareness and be still.

SUMMARY OF THE EIGHT COMMON HAPPENINGS

1. Memories

2. Abstract dreams

3. Millions of thoughts

4. Emotional energy

5. Physical sensations

6. Sleeps and meeps

7. Peace, love, joy and oneness

8. Still silent space

By highlighting the common meditation happenings, it is my hope that you are more willing to both let them happen and let them go whenever they do. For the more stubborn thoughts or uncomfortable emotions that may occur, I recommend you read the next two chapters to adopt the most optimal meditation mind-set, and also learn a recommended protocol for getting peace with any problematic thoughts, emotions or physical sensations, which may be harder to let go when using Mind Calm.

Chapter 9

OPTIMUM MEDITATION MIND-SET

Do you want mind calm or do you want every meditation to look and feel exactly how you think it should? Unfortunately, having preconceived ideas about what must happen when you meditate can lead to frustration and may make you want to quit before getting the results you want. To enjoy practising Mind Calm, I recommend that you embrace the three ideal attitudes outlined in this chapter. These attitudes become more important, not less, the more you meditate. Trust me, inadvertently it is easy to become rigid in your routine, and try to force specific happenings on your meditation practice to your mind's liking. It is natural to want to experience calm stillness when you meditate, but to develop peace with mind, it is vitally important that you adopt the following meditation mind-sets for all your open- and closed-eye Mind Calm practice.

THE MIND-SETS FOR MIND CALM

Mind-set 1: What's going to happen?

Once I was in a relationship with a woman who had a young child. When the little girl started walking, she would often come into my office, plant her feet firmly on the ground and with wide-open excited eyes say, 'What's going to happen?' I would turn to her with a big smile and similar wide-open eyes and say back to her, 'What's going to happen?' She'd then dance on the spot from sheer excitement and joy. To this day, I still remember fondly how wonderfully innocent she was and how her excitement for life was so contagious and enlivening.

When I started meditating more regularly I forgot her lessons in innocence and being curious. I forgot to be excited about not knowing what was going to happen. Instead, I started to try to force my will. I would sit down to meditate and without realizing, attempt to make my meditation look and feel how my mind thought it should. This quickly led to an inner struggle against anything that happened outside the parameters of my preconceived ideas about what the perfect meditation should be like. Instead of being innocently curious like a child, I would judge and resist what happened, which only made my meditations counterproductive and stressful.

Boredom would also creep into my meditations too, due to my lack of curiosity. Lacking an attitude of exploration and observation, I would give my attention to the commentator in my mind saying that I had so many other more fun and interesting things that I could be doing, rather than sitting with my eyes closed meditating.

Boredom is a by-product of not being present and lacking an attitude of 'What's Going to Happen?'

Whenever you are bored you have stopped being present and begun thinking. By shifting into a more curious mind-set, your meditation will immediately become more enlivening and enjoyable. You will find being curious is also a great way to be alert. The more alert you are (engaging GAAWO) the fewer thoughts you will naturally have and mind calm will abound.

Clock-watching

Hand in hand with boredom is clock-watching. When a person forgets to be fully engaged and curious, they can end up less attentive to what's happening now and more concerned with making sure they get through the 20- or 30-minute meditation sitting that they'd planned. This 'getting to the end' approach ends up missing the point of meditating, which is to savour the moment you're in.

Watch out for this common Time Trap. If you are clock-watching then you can be sure you're lacking the optimal mind-set for getting the most from meditation. Time really does fly when you're having fun. Take a moment to consider a hobby that you absolutely love. When engaged with your hobby, time disappears and hours can pass because of your total engrossment in the task at hand. The same can be the case for meditation. It need not be a means to an end or a monotonously dull daily routine that you do because you know you should. It can be a joy-filled adventure through timeless unbounded consciousness.

The choice between dullness and delight can be yours, by adopting a 'What's Going to Happen?' attitude.

Mind-set 2: Bring it OM!

Linking back to the common meditation happenings, without a mind-set of 'Bring It On' (or should I say, 'Bring It OM!'), then meditating can quickly become a struggle. For the best results, you need to be willing to let everything happen with unconditional allowing. Catch yourself if you ever sit down to meditate with any of the following intentions:

- I hope I don't have a busy Calm Sitting.

- I hope these uncomfortable emotions go away.

- I hope there're no external noises or distractions.

- I hope I don't fall asleep again.

- I hope I don't think about any bad memories.

- I hope no uncomfortable physical sensations happen.

The list can go on and on...

By being attached to how your meditation looks and resisting it when it doesn't go to your mind-made plan, you can end up in an inner struggle instead of serenity. You will fight the natural tendencies of your mind and body and become attached to things always being to your liking. Remember, attachment happens when you believe x, y or z will make you happier, peaceful, loved, etc. Attachment buys into the illusion that things need to change before you can enjoy these human pleasures. However, the reality of the situation is the exact opposite.

By letting go of needing things to be any fixed way, your mind becomes calmer and the lack of resistance allows for more enjoyable states of being to come to the forefront of your individual life experience.

Awareness of sound is a thought

When I first learned to meditate, I excitedly rushed home for my first private meditation. I recall sitting down on my brand new meditation cushion, lighting a candle and closing my eyes. Without a word of a lie, within a minute of me beginning, a really loud road drill started thumping away at the hard concrete outside my bedroom window! I immediately started judging and resisting the noise. I remember thinking: *This is so typical, I can't meditate with all this noise happening, I think I will stop for now and try again later*. Listening to my mind that day, I got up and walked away from a golden opportunity to practise being at peace with my thoughts about the noise.

> *Awareness of sound is a thought so let it go to return to the silence within.*

Instead of treating the sound as just another thought, I continued with my meditation journey believing I needed external quiet to find inner silence. As a result, I became irritated every time I noticed noises happening when I was trying to meditate. It turns out the same went for all the other mind-made rules that I'd picked up along the way with regards to how I could enjoy some peace. I believed I needed to stop my thoughts, be void of emotions, never be physically uncomfortable, and make my external life circumstances perfect, for peace to be possible. Hopefully by now, you can see this is not so. Engaged in such an approach, it's hard not to become controlling when trying to force your mind, body and life to be your idea of perfect so you can eventually enjoy some calm. However, the simple antidote to postponing your peace until things are different, better and improved is simply to adopt a mind-set of 'Bring It On'.

Now, if noise happens I let it. If thoughts want to float through my mind, I let them. If emotions are present in my body, I welcome them. And if I ever get physical sensations that my mind might judge as negative, I see the judgement and let my body do whatever it needs. If I've been lost in thinking for a few minutes, I don't look back to judge it, instead I take a moment to be grateful for being awake to the present moment once again.

Irrespective of what happens, the simple strategy for it not to be a problem is to let it go and keep GAAWOing.

Mind-set 3: Keep GAAWOing

Meditation works if you maintain a regular practice. Perhaps paradoxically, it is simultaneously a quick fix while also being a long-term winning strategy. Engaging GAAWO creates immediate mind calm, but if you want to make it a habit then you must keep doing it!

Your mind has loved being the centre of your attention and it might not accept relegation to the sidelines without a bit of a tantrum first. Be ready for your mind to say that you're too busy today to meditate or it's not working. Prepare yourself for your mind finding fault in the actual Mind Calm techniques too. It wants you to keep searching for the next technique and then the next. For the best results, commit to practise even if at times when you don't see the point.

I promise you that if you keep GAAWOing, then one year from now you will be experiencing so much more calm and contentment compared to if you don't get started or keep up your daily routine.

Let's face it, the next year is going to happen whether you meditate or not, so you may as well set yourself up for a much happier future by investing some time every day in your Mind Calm practice.

PERMANENT PEACE STARTS NOW

Desiring peace is natural and beautiful. The remarkable news is that enjoying peace for life is possible. Yet, despite this exciting possibility, always remember: life is only ever happening now, so peace for life is 100 per cent about being still now. If you want your experience of calm to be consistent then simply make it your number one priority to be inwardly attentive to still silent space now. Let the future take care of itself. The only thing that matters is where your attention is right now. Ask yourself: *Am I putting most of my attention on movement or stillness, sound or silence, stuff or space?* If you find yourself caring whether your mind calm is permanent or not, it means that your attention has slipped away from the presence of your consciousness now and gone into the future via your mind. Be here now. Be still now, and you will find that peace is permanently present – it always has been!

CALM NEVER LEFT YOU; YOU LEFT THE CALM!

Playing with Mind Calm consistently will help you to notice that you experience a sense of calm every time you become aware of the underlying still silent spacious reality of the present moment.

> *Your awareness is the permanent aspect to you and your awareness is still and calm.*

Beautifully, you can discover that peace never left you; rather, you left peace, simply by taking your attention away from this moment by engaging in thoughts, emotions, physical sensations and ever-changing life circumstances.

I encourage you to play fully with Mind Calm with the curiosity of a young child and be open to whatever happens. The result of saying 'Bring It On' to every aspect of human life is mind calm, love and heaps of happiness. Although 'Bring It On' is such a simple strategy for serenity, I cannot emphasize its importance enough. It's a master key to getting peace with your mind, peace with your emotions and ultimately peace with your life. So much so that it sits at the heart of the protocol that I'm going to share now for getting peace with any problem that you may encounter along your way...

Chapter 10

PEACE WITH MIND PROTOCOL

Getting peace with any problem is possible by healing your relationship with your mind's thoughts and emotions about the issue. Instead of working hard to change your mind to get peace with past events, current concerns or future fears, for example, you can be free now without having to engage in any intellectual convincing or therapy. Mind Calm and the principles that sit at the heart of the technique need not be used passively. On the contrary, it can be applied in a dynamic way for immediate relief from any problems that you may be currently facing.

Using my 'peace with mind' approach on specific issues requires a totally new mind-set compared to the more traditional therapeutic approaches available. Let's compare the therapy mind-set with Mind Calm:

Therapeutic mind-set	Mind Calm mind-set
There's something wrong with my life and me.	There is nothing wrong with consciousness (my real self).
I need to change, fix and improve my mind.	My relationship with my mind is what's important.
Problems happen that need to be resolved.	Problems are things that I've judged negatively.
Negative emotions are due to what happens.	Resistance to 'what is' causes negative emotions.
I need to get rid of my negative emotions.	There is no need to push away any emotions.

LIFE IS THE CONTEXT OF YOUR AWAKENING

Every moment of every day offers opportunities to wake up from your conditioned mind into a more consciously aware and liberated way of relating to life. Your inner state of calm is a great barometer, which provides instantaneous feedback on what you are unconsciously judging and resisting in your life versus what you're letting be and loving unconditionally. So if you're open to be taught by life and let go of out-of-date, mind-based habitual reactions, then your life will gently guide you towards a more conscious, free and loving way to be.

To love unconditionally is to be in harmony with what is.

With traditional therapy, the focus is on changing the mind, but with Mind Calm, a modern-day meditation model, it is all about changing your relationship with your mind. This more conscious-raising way of healing involves seeing your mind-made judgements about life, which are making things into problems, and then being willing to let go of the inner resistance that is making you feel bad.

When getting 'peace with mind' you do not need to engage in any kind of intellectual reasoning as to why you can be at peace with your past, present or future. Which, again, is different to the traditional therapeutic model, which usually involves talking or thinking at length about more positive ways of re-perceiving problematic people, events or things. With traditional therapy, if something 'bad' has happened, you will aim to find more positive ways to think about the problem so the mind can feel justified to be at peace with it. However, when getting 'peace with mind', this is not necessary. Instead your focus is entirely on seeing the judgemental thoughts in your mind that you are resisting. Remember, it is not what's happening that is a problem, but instead your thoughts and emotions about what's happening that are making things appear to be problems.

When you get peace with the thoughts and emotions that you are having about life, you then immediately get peace with what has happened, is happening and might happen in your life.

BEYOND THE 'FIX IT' THERAPY MODEL

With the intention of bringing meditation to life and making it a highly practical resource for people to use within a range of contexts, I teamed up with Sasha Allenby, co-author of the bestselling book *Matrix Reimprinting* (Hay House, 2010). Sasha and I started working together when we recognized a shared passion for offering an alternative approach to traditional therapy that could help people to let go of problems, but in a more consciously aware way.

Sasha and I both have therapeutic backgrounds (Sasha with Matrix Reimprinting and me with Mind Detox Method) and have helped thousands of people worldwide. Both of these techniques are very effective when it comes to changing the mind, letting go of trauma and getting peace with what's happened in the past. To this day, I still offer Mind Detox clinics and teach Mind Detox Practitioners via my Academy. (So, at no point am I saying that therapy is redundant and, if you feel that you could benefit from seeing a therapist, you might want to check out Sasha's Matrix Reimprinting or my *Heal the Hidden Cause* books to see if these modalities resonate with you). However, if you've done therapy, but still find yourself falling into old patterns, and are looking for the next step post-therapy, then I believe what I'm going to share now could be it.

A WAY FORWARD FROM POST-THERAPY LIMBO

Therapy can offer very useful interventions to resolves specific issues. If you have a problem then you can think through solutions and get into a better frame of mind. However, what next? I've met a lot of people who are experiencing what I call 'post-therapy limbo', whereby they have done lots of work on themselves and have got to the point where they feel there's more to personal growth than fixing and changing things, but don't know what. This is where the Reawakening Protocol, developed by Sasha and I, can offer a way forward.

The Reawakening Protocol, which in this book I also refer to as the 'Peace with Mind Protocol', is a non-therapeutic intervention that can be used to get peace with a specific problem from the Mind Calm mind-set outlined at the beginning of this chapter. Awakened is a term commonly used when referring to living in a consciously aware state of being. We use this protocol to wake up from the mind-based judgements and resistances through being consciously aware. It is always used alongside Mind Calm, but whereas Mind Calm is typically used in a more general way, the Reawakening Protocol provides precise steps on how to get peace with specific problems that you are feeling compelled to think about at length during daily life or Calm Sittings.

SOME THOUGHTS THINK THEY ARE SO SPECIAL

When going about your day or during your Calm Sittings, you may find that you come across some thoughts that are emotionally intense. They play havoc in your mind more than other thoughts, which you find easier to let go of with Mind Calm. They might be thoughts about your health, a friend or family member, or your financial situation, for example. 'Special thoughts' are ones that feel very personal and usually have emotions associated with them. They are thoughts that you tend not to see, but immediately start 'being', i.e. thinking about, whenever they pass through your awareness. For example,

- Am I with the right person?

- What if my body never gets better?

- What if something bad happens to my children?

- How am I going to pay the bills this month?

These are just some of the special thoughts that people can find it harder to let go of, to the point that if they were to sit down to meditate then they could end up thinking about their special thoughts for the majority of the time.

> *Special thoughts grab your attention and before you know it you can end up lost in thinking.*

Having had many people come to me with emotionally charged special thoughts like these, I have become very clear that it isn't always enough to just tell them to 'go home and meditate'. To do that would often set them up for uncomfortable Calm Sittings that could make them avoid meditating and, in some cases, cause them to quit for good. I don't want this for you. I want you to enjoy meditation and so I have co-created the following protocol that I recommend you use alongside Mind Calm on any of the more stubborn special thoughts that you may come across. You will find when using the Reawakening Protocol that your special thoughts stop feeling so special and as a result become easier to let go of when continuing with Mind Calm.

Before taking you through in detail this protocol for getting peace with mind, here is a quick summary so you can understand how it sits alongside Mind Calm.

The six-step Peace with Mind Protocol

1. Perceived Problem

State the problem that you want to heal your relationship with today.

2. Reality Check

Be here now by tuning in and noticing that this moment is happening.

3. Mind Made

Temporarily engage the story in your mind about the problem.

4. Resist Persist

Notice the 'special thought' you are resisting and where you feel it in your body.

5. Bring It On

Let the 'special thought' and feeling be present within you with no resistance.

6. Mind Calm Sitting

Play with 'seeing it, not being it' during a Calm Sitting.

From reading through the above six steps, you will see that you start by deciding upon the problem you want to heal your relationship with. You then have a reality check to tune in to now, put your attention on the context of this moment using GAAWO (see page 44) or by using the Noticing Now Space Mind Calm Game (see page 155).

Once you are fully present, you then temporarily leave the moment to go intentionally into your mind to start thinking about the problem. The reason for being present first is so that you see the movement away from the calm of now into the movement of your mind. (With time your desire to leave calm will diminish, but for now, continue with the protocol if it is a special thought that is demanding your attention). Once you've thought about the story for a short while (ideally no more than three minutes), you want to find which thought within the story has the most emotional intensity to it. This will be your special thought and the one that you are going to heal your relationship with.

When you know the special thought, you will take a moment to notice where you feel the thought in your body. Remember, if you are resisting the thought there will be negative emotion present. You will usually feel the thought in your stomach, solar plexus or chest, but it can be anywhere, so just trust your first answer. Then, when you know the special thought and location of the associated feelings, you turn your attention to letting go of inner resistance. This is done with the intention to 'bring it on' and by letting it be present within you. Having stopped resisting the thought and feeling, you will find the emotion ease and calm return (and in some cases, you may even find yourself laughing at the special thought). At this point, you can stop the protocol here or sit for a while using closed-eye Mind Calm.

Doing a Mind Calm sitting at this point allows you to practise seeing the story of the problem in your mind and letting it go by returning to GAAWO and your Calm Thoughts. Using Mind Calm can instil the habit of being at peace with the particular thoughts and emotions with which you had a problem.

Upon completing this procedure you will find that you will no longer feel compelled to think about the special thought. It will feel more neutral, and be easier to let go of and return to Mind Calm moving forward. Please remember, there is an important distinction between therapy and this meditative approach. You are not engaging in any intellectual reasoning in order to try to get peace with the problem. Instead, with this protocol, you are getting peace with the thoughts and emotions that you were having about the issue in your life.

> *By getting peace with your mind*
> *naturally, you get peace with your life.*

Pretty amazing stuff if you play with it! This alternative to therapy can help you get peace simply by seeing that the real cause of your suffering is unseen judgements and resistances. Using this protocol, you can observe the judgement thoughts and let go of resistance to return to inner calm immediately. Wow, imagine the possibilities!

PEACE WITH MIND PROTOCOL

Now you are aware of the six steps to get peace with any problem that is playing havoc with your Mind Calm, here follow the full instructions for the Reawakening Protocol Using Mind Calm Meditation.

IMPORTANT:

- Only use this protocol on your own if you are confident you can do so without the support of a qualified Reawakening Protocol Practitioner or Mind Calm Master Coach.

- If you find the protocol difficult then you could, if you preferred, put a temporary hold on using it until you have been practising Mind Calm meditation for a while and begun to cultivate the ability to be attentive to still silent consciousness.

Step 1: Perceived Problem

Without going into the story yet, briefly describe the problem with which you want to heal your relationship today.

Step 2: Reality Check

In order to for you to heal your relationship with this issue, start with a Reality Check by noticing that this moment is happening: *What can I currently see? What sounds can I hear? What am I physically touching?* To align your attention with now you can also use 'Noticing Now Space' (see page 155) or GAAWO (see page 44).

Once resting more aware of the present moment, you are in the optimum state to continue with the next step.

Step 3: Mind Made

Events become problems when you take your attention away from the present moment to think about them in your mind. If you want to stay calm, then stay present with context awareness. However, if you have a special thought that is demanding your attention and leading to the compulsion to overthink, then, for no longer than three minutes, leave this moment and intentionally engage the story in your mind about the problem.

Consider: *What is the problem? Why is it a problem? Ultimately, what is it about what happened, is happening or might happen that is the problem for me?*

Step 4: Resist Persist

Having been thinking about the story, now notice and take note of which of the thought(s) included in your story has the highest emotional intensity associated with it/them. The one with the highest emotional charge is the special thought that you are resisting. Remember, thousands of thoughts pass through your awareness every day, but when your special thought happens you immediately resist its existence. Therefore, it is your inner resistance to the special thought that is causing the stress and negative emotions you may be feeling.

Consider this: *What thought am I resisting most and where do I feel that thought in my body?*

Before moving on to the next step, make sure you have a specific special thought and the location in your body where you feel the thought.

Special thought + emotion in body.

Step 5: Bring it on

Now the good news: It is not what has happened, is happening or might happen that's the problem, but instead your relationship with your thoughts about these things that is determining how you are currently feeling. Remember, there has been an unseen judgement and resistance to the presence of the thoughts in your mind and emotions in your body that you need to see and let go of if you want to return to calm.

Consider this: *What happens when I say 'bring it on' to the thoughts and feelings?*

Watch the thoughts and emotions and let them be present with you – without resisting them. As you remain aware through watching, observe what happens to the thoughts and feelings when you say 'bring it on' to them (out loud or silently). If you are no longer resisting the thoughts and feelings with an attitude of 'bring it on', then their emotional intensity will subside, to be replaced with calmer and more light-hearted feelings.

Step 6: Mind Calm Sitting

Now you are going to sit for a while (from 5 to 15 minutes) in closed-eye meditation and play with seeing the stories in your mind about the problem.

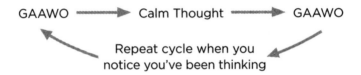

GAAWO ⟶ Calm Thought ⟶ GAAWO

Repeat cycle when you
notice you've been thinking

When using Mind Calm immediately after the Peace with Mind Protocol, be especially vigilant to any thoughts about the problem that you are healing your relationship with. Whenever you notice such thoughts, see them, don't be them. Return to GAAWO, use a Calm Thought, and re-engage GAAWO until you notice that you've been thinking about the story of the problem again, at which point repeat the three steps of Mind Calm.

A SILENT SOUL-UTION TO ANY PROBLEM

Anytime a special thought crops up, use this protocol to get peace with it and then return to your usual Mind Calm routine. Over time you will find that it becomes a very natural, almost instantaneous response within you whenever you start thinking about a problem. You will see the thought that you are resisting and where the associated emotion is in your body, then let go of any resistance by letting it be present within you.

TOP TIP 1: PICTURES ARE PERFECT

Occasionally your special thought will have an image associated with it. This image will be a visual representation of the thought. More often than not, the pictures that you mind will come up with will be extreme or exaggerated. For example,

- The image might be you homeless begging for money on the streets when thinking the special thought: *What if I lose everything?*

- The image might be you old, alone and lonely when thinking the special thought: *I will never meet anyone.*

- The image might be you looking in the mirror at a physically obese reflection of yourself when thinking the special thought: *I'm never going to lose weight.*

Upon noticing the image, use it in the same way you would any other thought. At Step 5: 'Bring It On', let the image be in your mind with no resistance. As usual, you will find the feelings associated with the image subside, you get peace with it and your mind will no longer bring it to your attention again (or if it does, it will be easy to let it go).

TOP TIP 2: THOUGHTS WITHIN THOUGHTS

Sometimes when using this protocol you may think you've found the special thought that you need to heal your relationship with but, as you start to move through the protocol, another more emotionally charged thought comes to mind. That is perfectly normal. If you find a deeper judgement thought that you are resisting, just move over to work on that special thought instead.

Part II

THE 10-PART MIND CALM PROGRAMME

INTRODUCTION TO THE 10-PART MIND CALM PROGRAMME

Liberate your Self by getting peace with your life. Move your attention away from inwardly judging and resisting how things are; being attached to making life look how you think it should; and overthinking about how you can fix, change and improve stuff. Instead, cultivate a calm and contented relationship with life that makes you happier, loving and, as a result, more successful. Mind Calm is a meditation practice to use every day, indefinitely. To get off to the best possible start, this 10-part programme provides a framework to get peace with the main aspects of your inner and outer life – including your thoughts, emotions, body, relationships, money, career, environment, society and life in general. By the time you've completed the programme, it is my hope that you'll be free to enjoy mind calm, irrespective of how each of the aspects of your life happens to be.

REMEMBER: YOU ARE FREE TO CHANGE WHATEVER YOU WANT

Just because you are at peace with how things are, it doesn't mean you cannot change things if that's what you want. The difference is that you'll no longer postpone feeling good until your life fits your mind-made rulebook of requirements. You enjoy the journey. You will make changes from an inner state of completeness and perfection and be able to see other people and world affairs through more compassionate eyes. Remember, the outer universe reflects the inner one. Peace on earth begins with you finding peace within your Self and a more loving world starts with you learning how to love unconditionally.

HOW THE MIND CALM PROGRAMME WORKS

Over the course of 10 weeks, or more quickly if you prefer, you will focus on bringing the 10 states of being included in the 10 Calm Thoughts (see page 90) into your conscious experience of life. For each part, you'll focus on one Calm Thought so that you can fully integrate it. I offer additional Mind Calm Games to play that can boost the benefits possible and also invite you to get peace with mind in relation to the key areas of life.

Commitment and the mind-set of persisting until you succeed can make getting what you want inevitable.

Now I appreciate that you might have limited spare time at your disposal, so the programme is designed to fit into a potentially busy schedule. To benefit fully, you need to be willing to invest 30–45 minutes per day in making mind calm your way of life. It is my hope that by now you are inspired to do this and can see the gigantic gains in doing so. Not only will you get more done with a clearer mind, but you will also find that your inner experience of life improves massively by making meditation a priority.

TOP TIP: FIT YOUR DAY AROUND MEDITATION

Due to the health and wellbeing benefits of meditation, I'd suggest that regular practice is up there in importance with eating, drinking and sleeping well. You wouldn't dream of not making time in your day to eat, drink and sleep, so why would you deprioritize meditation? Living without conscious awareness, you risk missing your day because you are distracted by your mind. You risk rushing around, from one thing to the next, while never fully enjoying and experiencing the precious life you've got. To increase the likelihood of completing the programme, I highly recommend you fit your day around meditation instead of trying to fit meditation into your day. This shift in priorities is the level of commitment you need to transform your relationship with your mind, for good.

Daily schedule for the 10-part Mind Calm Programme

Morning Mind Calm Sitting

Each day begins with a meditation entirely focused on the Calm Thought relating to the part of the programme you are in.

Daytime Mind Calm Game + Protocol

During the daytime there's a Mind Calm Game to play that explores being consciously aware. There's also a recommended topic for the Peace with Mind Protocol, so that you can transform your relationship with life during the 10-part programme.

Evening Mind Calm Sitting

The evening meditation includes all 10 Mind Calm Thoughts so that you can also continue cultivating all of the other states of being throughout the programme.

ABOUT THE MIND CALM THOUGHTS

The 10 Mind Calm Thoughts bring into your conscious awareness the living experience of the intentions that sit at the heart of each of them. Ancient spiritual teachers from numerous traditions have been known to say: 'You are what you seek.' Albeit rather confusing if you're not currently feeling peace, love, joy or whatever it is you happen to be 'seeking', these teachers were referring to the essence of consciousness, which in the awakened reality of the here and now, is these stunning states of being and more.

> *If you're not directly experiencing your exquisite being, then you are distracted by the content of your mind and life.*

The 10 Calm Thoughts are intentions; seeds that already exist within you. Engaging GAAWO and repeatedly bringing them into your awareness gives them the water, sunshine and air they need to grow into their fullest potential. The more you nurture the 10 seed intentions with your time and attention, the more you will be pleasantly surprised to notice them present within your experience of life.

It is best to work with the 10 Calm Thoughts intuitively and with a wide-open heart and mind. This is how they originally came through to me when I first intuited them. I didn't sit down and intellectually think them through logically. Instead, they came to me in an instant download when sitting in meditation. To use them with force, effort or control is to dilute their power and pollute their purity.

Avoid using them to push any human experience away, rather let them help you be at peace with whatever thoughts, emotions, physical sensations and life circumstances may be happening. Used with gentleness and openness, they act as real-time reminders of your heart's highest hope and give you the opportunity, when caught up in your mind, to make a more conscious choice – away from the mind-made version of reality to a more awakened awareness of the present moment.

The meaning of the 10 Calm Thoughts

In my personal experience, Mind Calm becomes more meaningful the more I meditate. During this programme I will share the meaning and purpose of each Calm Thought, along with what they can teach you. By sharing my personal meanings in this book, it is my hope that you will let your intuition reveal the living wisdom present within each of the 10 Calm Thoughts. I'm excited to learn what you will discover!

ABOUT THE MIND CALM GAMES

During the programme you will have a series of Mind Calm Games to play. Most of the games are best engaged with your eyes open and used alongside any other activities you are doing at the time. They help to cultivate the habit of being consciously aware throughout your day.

Some of these games will resonate with you and you will find that they work almost immediately. Others might not make any sense, or you may find them more difficult. My advice is to give each of the 10 Mind Calm Games a good outing. By actively playing with them you will make some amazing discoveries and, more importantly, you will make massive shifts in your unconscious thinking to a new and improved habit of present moment awareness.

TOP TIP: THE THREE GOLDEN RULES

There are three golden rules for all of the Mind Calm Games that you must adhere to, if you want to reap the immediate benefits:

1. **You can't play the game wrong.** So just play like a child. I remember as a kid I used to play for hours with a cardboard box and a couple of spoons, imagining that I was in a boat. I couldn't do it 'wrong' because I was just playing. So don't try to get them right, just play and explore innocently and see what happens.

2. **You can't do them later.** You can only do the games now so don't try to analyse what you're doing or plan to do them later if you like the sound of them. Instead, just do them, immediately.

3. **You can't think about doing them.** You can only actively engage them. If they aren't working for you, then you can be sure that you are in your mind thinking about them, instead of being in the moment experiencing what I'm inviting you to notice.

ABOUT THE PEACE WITH MIND PROTOCOL

The Peace with Mind Protocol was explained in Chapter 10 (see page 121). During this programme, I'd encourage you to use it on specific issues in your life that you are currently judging and resisting as negative, bad, wrong or worse. Areas of interest to get peace with include:

- Your body

- Emotions

- Relationships

- Career

- Environment

- Your past and future

- Your potential for success

- Society

By working through them one by one, you will arrive at the end of the programme with a more peaceful relationship with your life and be free to live without feeling something is wrong – which is what a successful life feels like.

1

CONNECTION

DAILY SCHEDULE

MORNING MIND CALM SITTING
OM CONNECTION (Soles of Feet) Calm Thought only
(Recommended duration: 10–15 minutes or longer if you have the time.)

DAYTIME MIND CALM GAME
Reality Check: Tune in to your senses to notice now

DAYTIME PEACE WITH MIND PROTOCOL
Get peace with aspects of your BODY that you don't like

EVENING MIND CALM SITTING
Use all 10 Calm Thoughts
(Recommended duration: 10–15 minutes or longer if you have the time.)

CALM THOUGHT

OM Connection (Soles of Feet)

Calm Thought Meaning: Everything in the cosmos is connected. You are connected to the Earth, the air you breathe, the food you eat, the water you drink, the nature you live within, the people on all corners of this planet and all living organisms both seen and unseen. Connection sits at the heart of consciousness and all existence.

Calm Thought Purpose: Getting too caught up in your mind causes you to lose connection with the Earth, become imbalanced, feel isolated and be less effective in the world. Being less engaged in the mind often leads to an awakening to the intricate interconnectedness of everything and everyone in the universe that, when known and experienced, radically transforms your relationship with your Self and life itself.

Calm Thought Focus: Feeling your feet is a very simple way of drawing your attention downwards to be less in your mind and more grounded. Using OM CONNECTION while focusing on the 'Soles of your Feet' helps you connect with Mother Earth's healing and transformative powers. You find that you begin to really appreciate the beauty of the physical world and your connection to it. This is also a great Calm Thought to start any Calm Sitting, as it gets you out of your busy head and into body awareness, and acts as a great way of connecting to the meditation you are about to do.

MIND CALM GAME

Reality Check – tune in to your senses to notice now

The more you are in the moment the less you are in your mind and the quieter it naturally becomes. Furthermore, as you become actively aware of what is happening now, you experience the still silent fragrance of what your awareness is like. This Reality Check involves taking your attention to your senses to fully see, feel, hear, smell and taste whatever is occurring right now. For this game, there are the full instructions and also a quick-start version if you are on the move and don't want to explore sensory awakening in detail, but still want to get some super cool and calming results.

Quick-start instructions

Visual: Notice an object that is currently in your field of vision that you were unaware of previously.

Audio: Notice a sound that is currently occurring in your proximity that you were unaware of previously.

Touch: Notice something that you are physically touching that you were unaware of previously.

Becoming attentive to these new visual, auditory and kinaesthetic things in your immediate environment can cause your mind to become calm.

Full sensory awakening instructions

Notice what you can see: Only look, without labelling. Look at the colours. Look at the shapes. Look at the textures.

Notice the light. Look at the distance between objects. Be aware of the space. Focus on individual objects, noticing things about them that you may have missed previously.

Notice what you feel: Now notice all that you are touching. Notice your clothes, the ground and the chair, if you are sitting on one. Feel the air dancing all around you. Feel the temperature. Notice how it feels to breathe. Feel life inside and around you. Just feel.

Now listen to the sounds: Tune in. Avoid labelling or judging. Just listen. Be super-stereo, tuning into sounds that you may have been missing previously. Are there birds or traffic in the distance? Is there a ticking clock? Or can you hear the sound of the air travelling up and down your nostrils? Tune in and listen as if the volume has been turned all the way up.

Now notice the smells: Take your attention to your nose by feeling the air as it enters your nostrils. Simply being fully aware of the air moving in and out of your nose can be an extremely enjoyable experience if you are fully attentive and involved in each breath. While you are at it, focus fully on what you can smell right now. Is the smell sharp or dull, high or low, sweet or sour? Take your attention to your nose and notice how your mind becomes clearer when you do so.

Now notice the tastes: Void of food, what tastes are already present within your mouth? Also play with sensory awakening with different foods and drinks. Totally tune in to your taste buds, the textures of the food and, of course, how it tastes. What it is like to hold the liquid temporarily in your mouth before you swallow? How does the food feel between your teeth as you chew? The simplest foods and drinks can be the most delicious experience if you eat consciously.

By filling your attention with your senses you leave less attention for the thinking mind. Naturally you think less and become more fulfilled with whatever you are seeing, hearing, feeling, smelling and tasting.

PEACE WITH MIND PROTOCOL

Get peace with your body

Use the Peace with Mind Protocol to heal your relationship with aspects of your body, including:

- Shape
- Weight
- Flaws
- Illness(es)
- Food
- Habits
- Fitness
- Energy levels

Using the above list for inspiration, consider what you currently perceive to be a problem relating to your body. Then use the Peace with Mind Protocol to get peace with the thoughts and emotions that you are having about a specific issue relating to your body.

The six-step Peace with Mind Protocol

1. Perceived Problem

State the problem that you want to heal your relationship with today.

2. Reality Check

Be here now by tuning in and noticing that this moment is happening.

3. Mind Made

Temporarily engage the story in your mind about the problem.

4. Resist Persist

Notice the 'special thought' you are resisting and where you feel it in your body.

5. Bring It On

Let the 'special thought' and feeling be present within you with no resistance.

6. Mind Calm Sitting

Play with 'seeing it, not being it' during a Calm Sitting.

For example, you might notice that you regularly resist the shape of your body. To use the protocol, consider what it is about the shape of your body that you don't like. Your first thought might be: *I'm fat* or *I'm too big* or *I'm too skinny*. Once you are clear on the special thought, notice where you feel it in your body. Then progress to the 'Bring It On' part of the protocol by letting the thought and emotion be present within you.

Doing so will reduce your mind's resistance to it and the emotion will subside accordingly, making the thought less personal. By all means, at this point, continue to do whatever you can to lose or gain weight if it is healthier to do so, but you will be more at peace with your current body shape while you go about making whatever changes you desire.

2

POWER

DAILY SCHEDULE

MORNING MIND CALM SITTING
OM POWER (Base of Spine) Calm Thought only
(Recommended duration: 10–15 minutes or longer if you have the time.)

DAYTIME MIND CALM GAME
Noticing Now Space: See the context of still silent space

DAYTIME PEACE WITH MIND PROTOCOL
Get peace with your POTENTIAL to succeed

EVENING MIND CALM SITTING
Use all 10 Calm Thoughts
(Recommended duration: 10–15 minutes or longer if you have the time.)

CALM THOUGHT

OM Power (Base of Spine)

Calm Thought Meaning: You are much more powerful than you may think. Living within you now exists the same power that moves the oceans, grows the forests and transports the planets. It is the driving force that gives birth to everything in creation.

Calm Thought Purpose: Identifying too strongly with your mind by believing all of its opinions about your capabilities, how confident you are and how impactful you can be, often leads to feelings of powerlessness or actions driven by ego-based ruthlessness. Depending on your beliefs, on one end of the power spectrum, you can end up timid, scared of engaging life fully, hide away and never live the purpose for which you were born. At the other end of the power spectrum, you can end up headstrong, driven by fear (although you wouldn't want to admit it!), end up forever forcing your will and pursue your best interests without concern for the impact on others or the world you live in. Somewhere in between these two points is a balanced power, based in love and the joy of exploration through creation.

Calm Thought Focus: Using OM POWER with your focus point at the 'Base of your Spine', can help you to find the inner source of all power and then use it wisely for the benefit of yourself, all of humanity and the world you live in.

MIND CALM GAME

Noticing Now Space – see the context of still silent space

As you are reading this I am going to assume you have a page in front of you, either printed or on a reading device. I want you to keep looking at the page as you notice your left shoulder. To notice it you don't need to look at it or move it, just tune in and notice your left shoulder. OK? Easy? Perfect.

Let's continue. Now notice your right foot. Again, keep looking ahead at the page as you notice your right foot. You can keep reading. You don't need to wiggle your toes or anything like that. You can simply take your attention to your right foot and notice it now. OK? Still easy? Great. Let's continue.

Now, without trying to figure out what I'm asking you to do, I want you to notice the space between you and this page. Just do that now. You don't have to look around between you and the page, just keep looking ahead and simply notice that the space exists. It's been there the entire time; all you are doing is noticing that it is there as you continue to keep your gaze on the page. Still easy? OK, let's continue playing.

Now I want you to notice the space around the page. Don't look directly around the page; keep looking directly ahead as you notice this space. Notice the space around the page for a few moments before continuing. You are doing great.

Now I want you to notice the space in the entire room. Like a switch in your awareness, let your attention notice the space in the entire room. As you do that, I want you to notice what it's like to do this.

What's your inner experience as you notice the space in the entire room? Remember, keep your gaze forward and don't look around the room trying to find or see the space. Trust me, it is there. All I want you to do is notice the space in the room. As you continue to do this, what word or words could you use to describe your inner experience, as you notice the space now?

I've asked literally hundreds of people to do this. Common answers include 'calm', 'peaceful', 'still', 'open', 'expansive', 'light', 'comforting', 'home' and 'freeing'. As you notice the space in the entire room, what word(s) could you use to describe what it's like to notice the space? Don't stop noticing the space to try to describe it as that will start you thinking and stop you experiencing. Just notice and trust your first words.

Let's continue. Now I want you to notice that this moment is happening. That you are sitting where you are, reading this word. Observing this word being read. And now this word. Simply notice that this moment is happening. What's it like to notice quietly? To do nothing except gently watch this moment occurring. What words could you use to describe your inner experience as you do this? Common words used to describe this are 'calm', 'peaceful', 'quiet', 'still', 'spacious', 'open' and 'free'.

Using this marvellous Mind Calm Game you can begin to cultivate context awareness, which is very similar to conscious awareness.

PEACE WITH MIND PROTOCOL

Get peace with your potential

Use the Peace with Mind Protocol to heal your relationship with your power and potential, including:

- Ability to succeed

- Fear of failure

- Out-of-reach goals

- Making changes

- Taking actions

- Personal limitations

- Confidence

- Self-esteem

Using the above list as inspiration, consider what you currently perceive to be a problem relating to your power and potential. Now use the Peace with Mind Protocol to get peace with the thoughts and emotions that you have about a specific issue relating to your potential to succeed.

The six-step Peace with Mind Protocol

1. Perceived Problem
State the problem that you want to heal your relationship with today.

2. Reality Check
Be here now by tuning in and noticing that this moment is happening.

3. Mind Made

Temporarily engage the story in your mind about the problem.

4. Resist Persist

Notice the 'special thought' you are resisting and where you feel it in your body.

5. Bring It On

Let the 'special thought' and feeling be present within you with no resistance.

6. Mind Calm Sitting

Play with 'seeing it, not being it' during a Calm Sitting.

For example, let's say you have noticed that you feel your goals are out of reach. To use the protocol, you want to consider what thoughts you are having in relation to not being able to achieve your goals. Maybe you have the thought, *I will never be able to do X*. You then want to notice where you feel that thought in your body, before 'bringing it on' by letting both the thought and emotion be present within you with no resistance. You will find the energy surrounding the thought disperses and will no longer feel so true.

Liberation from self-judgemental thoughts and resistances like this can free you up to harness your inner power to fulfil your potential.

3
JOY

DAILY SCHEDULE

MORNING MIND CALM SITTING
OM JOY (Navel) Calm Thought only
(Recommended duration: 10–15 minutes or longer if you have the time.)

DAYTIME MIND CALM GAME
Inward Gazing: Be inwardly attentive towards your heart

DAYTIME PEACE WITH MIND PROTOCOL
Get peace with EMOTIONS that you judge as negative

EVENING MIND CALM SITTING
Use all 10 Calm Thoughts
(Recommended duration: 10–15 minutes or longer if you have the time.)

CALM THOUGHT

OM Joy (Navel)

Calm Thought meaning: Joy is the natural expression of life. It is the creative juice of the universe. Joy is beyond the temporary highs of happiness. Letting go of judgement, resistance, attachment and the past and future allows joy to be consciously present. It is the natural by-product of being thankful for one's existence.

Calm Thought purpose: Growing up, it is common to mislabel joy for fear, angst or anxiety and end up suppressing its transformative powers. Joy is the flow of inner-life-infused energy existing in everyone. By letting go of the mind-made labels about emotional energies and letting emotions be present within you with zero resistance, you can find that feelings you once knew as anxiety or fear have always been joy's powerful presence. Furthermore, although we are taught we need things to make us happy, joy is beyond mind-based reasoning. In the pursuit of happiness by fixing, changing and improving circumstances, many miss a glorious gift in being born human, which is to experience joy for no reason. Joy is ever-present to those awake to its on-going presence.

Calm Thought Focus: Using 'OM JOY' with your attention in the 'Navel' can help to heal your relationship with this potent force for good within you and let the energetic celebration of existence carry you on its wondrous wings.

MIND CALM GAME

Inward Gazing – be inwardly attentive towards your heart

This game helps you to let energy be present within you. What is it like if you pretend to have double-sided eyes and look outwards while gazing inwards towards your heart at the same time?

Instructions

- Find something outside and in front of you that you can use as an external point of focus. This might be a door handle, the corner of a picture frame or a spot on the wall.

- Then, while maintaining some attention outwards on that external point of reference, pretend that you have double-sided eyes and look back, in and down towards your heart area or towards where you are feeling a negative emotion (usually your stomach, solar plexus or heart area).

- As you do this, notice what happens to the thoughts in your mind. Do they quieten? Do you become aware of how still it is within you now? If you are watching an emotion in your body somewhere, notice what happens to its intensity as you 'see it, don't be it'. Does it dissolve? Are you able to be at peace with it being present within you?

Inward gazing is a fantastic way of cultivating a more consistent inward attentiveness. You will find that you can take your attention inwards and place it upon your heart, and still interact very effectively with the external world. In fact, many people who practise this technique find that they become more present than when all of their attention is outwards on stuff, sound and movement. Play with inward gazing when speaking with friends, working at your computer and walking in nature. It can help you to become aware of the presence of peace within, as well as hone your skills at context awareness.

PEACE WITH MIND PROTOCOL

Get peace with your emotions

After a couple years of meditating regularly, I reluctantly went to my meditation teacher to tell him I didn't think it was working. My reasoning was the simple fact that I was still feeling intense emotions in my body that were uncomfortable. Sometimes feeling as if my solar plexus were on fire with feelings, I would meditate often but it didn't appear to be getting any better.

Upon hearing that I was trying to make them go away, he compassionately challenged me, 'When did I tell you to try to get rid of your emotions? You are a human being with a body that will always have energy within it. If you want to enjoy true peace, then you must learn how to be at peace with how you feel.'

Peace is not the absence of emotions. So, by learning to let them be present within you, you can discover a calm stillness present alongside all movement. To explore this for yourself, use the Peace with Mind Protocol to heal your relationship with any emotions that you might habitually judge as negative and therefore resist, including:

- Anger
- Anxiety
- Fear
- Sadness
- Guilt
- Hurt

Using the above list as inspiration, consider what emotions you currently perceive to be negative and problematic. Then use the Peace with Mind Protocol to get peace with the emotional energies so that you can either let them go or harness their power for good.

The six-step Peace with Mind Protocol

1. Perceived Problem

State the problem that you want to heal your relationship with today.

2. Reality Check

Be here now by tuning in and noticing that this moment is happening.

3. Mind Made

Temporarily engage the story in your mind about the problem.

4. Resist Persist

Notice the 'special thought' you are resisting and where you feel it in your body.

5. Bring It On

Let the 'special thought' and feeling be present within you with no resistance.

6. Mind Calm Sitting

Play with 'seeing it, not being it' during a Calm Sitting.

For example, let's say you tend to feel anxious when thinking about public speaking. You want to consider what it is about public speaking that makes you feel that way. This might be 'everyone looks at me' or 'I might make a fool of myself', etc. Using the Peace with Mind Protocol you will notice where you feel the most special thought in your body. Then see what happens when you let the thought and feeling be present within you with zero resistance. Having shifted into the 'bring it on' mind-set, you will find the emotional energy stops being problematic and the thought of public speaking, for example, is no longer a scary situation that you would feel the need to avoid.

By doing this protocol with emotions you tend to judge as negative, you can enjoy more emotional liberation. Remember, it is not the things in life that we fear or necessarily want to avoid, but the way we believe these things will make us feel. Getting peace with your emotions about life therefore enables you to harness the power of your emotions and frees you up to engage life fully.

4

PEACE

CALM THOUGHT

OM Peace (Solar Plexus)

Calm Thought meaning: Consciousness is peaceful. Or said another way, consciousness is full of peace. Everything happens within the constant context of still silent spacious consciousness that is inherently calm. All movement happens within peace, including the natural flow of joy within. All noise can only be distinguished and heard due to the context of silent serenity, and all stuff is filled up with and fills peace-filled consciousness.

Calm Thought purpose: Trying to find peace by stopping your mind, body and life doesn't work. Pushing against the natural flow of these aspects of being human actually causes stress. Only when you learn to rest back, let go and just be... do you notice the presence of peace that remains. You see how it actually takes vast amounts of effort and energy not to be peaceful. Being distracted by thoughts and emotions can lead to the impression that peace is not present. However, being consciously aware and, more importantly, noticing what it is experientially like to be aware, you find the oasis of calm within.

Calm Thought Focus: Most people experience emotions in their solar plexus area, so by using 'OM PEACE' with your attention in your 'Solar Plexus', you can heal your relationship with any movement in your mind, body and life – to rest in perfect peace, while fully engaging life.

MIND CALM GAME

Heart Watching – look out at life from your heart

One easy and fun way to gain immediate mind calm is a game I call 'Heart Watching'. This game draws your attention further inwards – naturally making you more consciously aware. With practice, it can help you to engage life with an inward attentiveness to the still silent presence within, as you go about your day.

Instructions

- Although your eyes are clearly on your face, this game encourages you to notice what it is also like to look out from the centre of your chest in your heart area.

- As you continue to read these words, notice what it is like to look out not only from the eyes on your face but also to look out at these words from your heart centre.

- Continuing to be attentive in this way a little longer, how would you describe your inner experience?

Common answers include 'calm', 'still', 'quiet', 'present' and so on. What is it like for you to engage Heart Watching by looking out from your heart area? It is fun to play this game with objects or with people you know. You can do it by facing each other and intending to look out at each other from your individual heart areas; it can lead to more Mind Calm and kindness.

PEACE WITH MIND PROTOCOL

Get peace with your environment

Being in one place while wishing you were somewhere else causes discontentment and limits your ability to see the beauty that is always present. Use the Peace with Mind Protocol to heal your relationship with your living and working environments, including:

- Home

- Workplace

- City

- Country

- Nature

- Earth health

Using the above list as inspiration, consider what you currently perceive to be a problem relating to your environment. Then use the Peace with Mind Protocol to get peace with the thoughts and emotions that you are having about a specific issue relating to where you live and work and the world you live in.

The six-step Peace with Mind Protocol

1. Perceived Problem

State the problem that you want to heal your relationship with today.

2. Reality Check

Be here now by tuning in and noticing that this moment is happening.

3. Mind Made

Temporarily engage the story in your mind about the problem.

4. Resist Persist

Notice the 'special thought' you are resisting and where you feel it in your body.

5. Bring It On

Let the 'special thought' and feeling be present within you with no resistance.

6. Mind Calm Sitting

Play with 'seeing it, not being it' during a Calm Sitting.

For example, you might be unhappy with the home you live in. You might think it's too small, too cluttered or have some other problem. If you see from this exercise that you are resisting the size, then you would want to notice what thoughts you are having about it. If *I cannot breathe in this tiny place* comes to mind for instance, then notice where you feel that thought in your body. Then go on to engage the 'bring it on' mind-set in relation to these thoughts and emotions until you notice more mind calm.

Remember, it is not the size of home that is making it hard to breathe, but your resistance to the thoughts you are having about the size of your home. By 'seeing it, not being it' you can be more content with where you are and not buy into the mind-made postponement that you can't be happy until you move. You can be happy, by moving from a mind-set of judgement and resistance to one of peace.

5

LOVE

DAILY SCHEDULE

MORNING MIND CALM SITTING
OM LOVE (Heart Centre) Calm Thought only
*(Recommended duration: 10–15 minutes or longer if you
have the time.)*

DAYTIME MIND CALM GAME
Loving Pink Light: Heal the part of you that is them

DAYTIME PEACE WITH MIND PROTOCOL
Get peace with your RELATIONSHIPS

EVENING MIND CALM SITTING
Use all 10 Calm Thoughts
*(Recommended duration: 10–15 minutes or longer if you
have the time.)*

CALM THOUGHT

OM Love (Heart Centre)

Calm Thought Meaning: Consciousness is love. It is an all-embracing all-allowing state of being within you. Love can never leave you because it is the fragrance of your very being. Love is beyond all of the conditional thought judgements, and needs no mind-based justifications or reasoning. Love is your true nature and is always present to be savoured by being shared.

Calm Thought Purpose: Mainstream media and modern-day schools of thought can give the impression that love is earned. You cannot love yourself or be loved by others until you live up to some criteria, suggesting that your personality, body, career, social life, etc., need to be a certain way for you and them to be deemed loveable. This isn't true. Conditional love like this is not love. Love is non-conditional and non-judgemental. It is therefore beyond the opinions of the mind and has no requirements or rules. Love is the natural by-product of letting go of the mind and returning to the essence of your being.

Calm Thought Focus: Using OM LOVE with the focus point in your 'Heart Centre' can help you to let go of believing that you need to do, prove or be better before you can be loveable, allowing you to express love to yourself, others and the world without being attached to getting anything in return.

MIND CALM GAME

Pink Loving Light – heal the part of you that is them

This technique is ancient in origin and can be used to heal relationships. It is used to heal all pain and suffering between the user and the subject by healing your inner resistance towards yourself and others. When using the Pink Loving Light game you are, in essence, healing the part of you that is them – which makes much more sense when you appreciate we are all ultimately one consciousness having multiple human experiences.

Instructions

1. Close your eyes and engage GAAWO.

2. Get yourself in a loving space. Remember a time when you felt loved or experienced love.

3. In your mind's eye, picture pink loving light radiating from your heart, encompassing you in a pink sphere.

4. Stay within your pink light sphere. Remember a most loving memory of yourself (this could be recent or from your childhood) and project this aspect of you outside the pink light sphere. Cover this projection of yourself with the pink loving light, still radiating from your heart.

5. Then, starting with your immediate family – mother, father, siblings, partner, children – imagine them appearing individually in front of you, outside the pink light sphere. If possible, make it an image of them in a loving memory. In your mind's eye, picture yourself covering each of them with the pink light as if you were icing a cake. Cover them with light and then let them go and move on to the next person. If there is someone who you cannot remember as part of a loving memory, just picture him or her in front of you. If you cannot do this, visualize bringing them in to stand at a distance and/or facing away from you.

6. Next, do this with anyone with whom you still have an emotional charge or discomfort.

7. Allow for anyone else to show up (whether you know them or not), cover him or her with the pink loving light and let them go as well.

In the beginning, this process should take no more than 10 minutes a day, eventually getting down to five minutes. If you can't visualize the pink light, that's fine, as it is the intent that's important. Once someone is gone, assume that they are finished for the day. You will get a sense of when someone is 'complete' and no longer requires the pink-light treatment. Some people will not show up for a while; others, who you didn't expect to see, will suddenly appear to receive their pink light.

This technique has been highly successful with people who have been raped, molested or abused. Runaway children have been known to reconnect with their family within weeks of starting to use it. Although most people using this technique find it easy to do, some can have difficulty with step 3. Be gentle on yourself and enjoy the results.

PEACE WITH MIND PROTOCOL

Get peace with your relationships

Use the Peace with Mind Protocol to heal your relationship with your relationships, including:

- Past partners

- Current partner

- Family

- Friends
- Colleagues
- Anyone you dislike

Aspects of your individual relationships you might also want to heal your relationship with include:

- Sex and intimacy
- Different opinions
- Common interests
- Tastes in food
- Conflicting habits
- Social preferences

Using the above list as your inspiration, consider what you currently perceive to be a problem relating to your relationships. Then use the Peace with Mind Protocol to get peace with the thoughts and emotions that you are having about a specific issue relating to relationships.

The six-step Peace with Mind Protocol

1. Perceived Problem
State the problem that you want to heal your relationship with today.

2. Reality Check
Be here now by tuning in and noticing that this moment is happening.

3. Mind Made

Temporarily engage the story in your mind about the problem.

4. Resist Persist

Notice the 'special thought' you are resisting and where you feel it in your body.

5. Bring It On

Let the 'special thought' and feeling be present within you with no resistance.

6. Mind Calm Sitting

Play with 'seeing it, not being it' during a Calm Sitting.

For example, let's say you are resisting a relationship break-up. Every time you think about the person you feel sad that you are no longer together. First, you want to decide the thought that you are resisting most about the split, which could be, *Without them I'm nobody* – remember the mind tends to exaggerate! You would then notice where you feel that thought in your body when you think it. Then go on to let the thought and emotion be present within you with no resistance and a 'bring it on' mind-set. Remember, you are not saying 'bring it on' to the fact that you split up, but to the thought you are having about the split.

By getting peace with your thoughts about your relationships, you can be at peace with past, current and possible future relationships. Mind calm around relationships can also help you to live in a less attached way, and not be dependent on others to feel loved, and as a result, enjoy more unconditional love.

6

TRUTH

DAILY SCHEDULE

MORNING MIND CALM SITTING
OM TRUTH (Throat) Calm Thought only
*(Recommended duration: 10-15 minutes or longer if you
have the time.)*

DAYTIME MIND CALM GAME
Silence Speaks: Be aware of the silence allowing sound

DAYTIME PEACE WITH MIND PROTOCOL
Get peace with your CAREER

EVENING MIND CALM SITTING
Use all 10 Calm Thoughts
*(Recommended duration: 10-15 minutes or longer if you
have the time.)*

CALM THOUGHT

OM Truth (Throat)

Calm Thought meaning: Truth is true whether you believe it is or not. Truth is absolute and eternal and exists beyond the confines of mind-made concepts. Truth can be known conceptually, but only ever awakens to its transformative healing powers through the direct living experience of an enlivened soul.

Calm Thought purpose: If given a choice, most people would choose to know the truth rather than live a lie. Despite this, many live a life full of false truths because they think their mind-made beliefs are absolutely true, when in most cases they're not. One person can believe one thing while another person can believe the exact opposite. Both may appear correct, relatively speaking, but both can be living an illusion of relative rightness. Beliefs are only ever relatively true. Truth, on the other hand, is true for everyone and in all time and space, in the same way as you don't need to believe in gravity for your feet to remain on the ground. Or you don't need to believe in the moment for it to be present always. Truth does not need the mind for it to exist. It just is.

Calm Thought Focus: Using OM Truth with your attention in your 'Throat' can help you to tune in and reconnect with the living truth of any given situation. You can be real and honest with yourself or others, and burn up ignorance and self-deception to awaken to real reality.

MIND CALM GAME

Silence Speaks – be aware of the silence allowing sound

Before I discovered context awareness I'd always thought there was only either 'noisy' or 'quiet', but, in reality, for there to be any sound there has to be silence at the same time. Sound odd? It did when I was first told this, but it's true if you can be attentive enough to hear the silence. Inner silence is something so familiar that it is easy to forget that it's present all the time. Children know it well, adults less so, because of being so distracted by the content of sounds.

Take a moment to consider this: if there were the context of noise, would you be able to hear anything? Or do you need silence for sound to exist? Even if you were at a rock concert and the music was so loud that you knew your ears were going to ting the following day, for you to hear the sound of the music there must be the constant existence of silence. Otherwise the context would be noise and you wouldn't be able to hear anything! The truth is that there is a constant underlying presence of silence that allows you to hear sounds, and that silence resides within you.

Instructions

1. One of the easiest places to locate the silence is within your ears. Take your attention to any sound you can hear right now and gently begin to notice that there is an inner silence that enables you to hear it.

2. Focus less on what you can hear. Instead, turn your attention to the one within you that is listening.

Gently be aware of the listener within to find the presence of now.

3. Another way of noticing silence is to locate your attention at the centre of your skull, then slowly move your attention outwards towards your ears.

For some people, there is a moment when they notice the silence; it becomes clear and blatantly obvious. Playing with putting your attention on the silence within you is a highly effective way of withdrawing your attention from your thinking mind and placing it instead on the context. As you feel what you focus on, focusing on silence helps you to feel more serene.

PEACE WITH MIND PROTOCOL
Peace with career

When you live your truth you naturally live your purpose. For this part of the programme, you are going to use the Peace with Mind Protocol to heal your relationship with any issues surrounding your career, including:

- Position

- Progress

- Workload

- Pressures

- Income

- Boredom

- Redundancy

- Competition

Using the above list as inspiration, consider what you currently perceive to be a problem relating to your career. Then use the Peace with Mind Protocol to bring peace to the thoughts and emotions that you are having about a specific issue relating to your work and living your purpose.

The six-step Peace with Mind Protocol

1. Perceived Problem

State the problem that you want to heal your relationship with today.

2. Reality Check

Be here now by tuning in and noticing that this moment is happening.

3. Mind Made

Temporarily engage the story in your mind about the problem.

4. Resist Persist

Notice the 'special thought' you are resisting and where you feel it in your body.

5. Bring It On

Let the 'special thought' and feeling be present within you with no resistance.

6. Mind Calm Sitting

Play with 'seeing it, not being it' during a Calm Sitting.

For example, let's say you are fearful of being made redundant. When you consider why you are concerned about it, you notice the thought happening in your mind – *I'm scared that I won't be able to get another job* – and feel that thought in your stomach. You will then see what happens when you let the thoughts and emotions occur without resisting them being in your mind and body. After a few moments of 'seeing the thought, not being the thought' you might find the feelings of fear are reduced, allowing you to continue your work with more Mind Calm. Not only will this allow you to perform at your best (making you an even more valuable member of the team), but also you will continue free from concern.

7

CLARITY

DAILY SCHEDULE

MORNING MIND CALM SITTING
OM CLARITY (Forehead Centre) Calm Thought only
*(Recommended duration: 10–15 minutes or longer if you
have the time.)*

DAYTIME MIND CALM GAME
Enlightened Eye: Look out from the centre of your skull

DAYTIME PEACE WITH MIND PROTOCOL
Get peace with aspects of SOCIETY that trouble you

EVENING MIND CALM SITTING
Use all 10 Calm Thoughts
*(Recommended duration: 10–15 minutes or longer if you
have the time.)*

CALM THOUGHT

OM clarity (Forehead Centre)

Calm Thought meaning: Confusion comes from having a busy mind and thinking too much. The contradictory nature of the mind – whereby one moment it can produce thoughts on one thing and thoughts on the complete opposite the next minute – makes true clarity very difficult from the surface of the mind. Clarity comes from stillness through being consciously aware.

Calm Thought purpose: Clarity creates the optimum inner platform for performing at your best. Without clarity, you aren't fully present and end up distracted by mental activity that can be both limiting and confusing. Relying on the mind for clarity can be a lost cause, especially if you remember the mind operates by jumping from polar opposites – and often everything in between – using the Judgement Game. *What ifs*, *buts* and *maybes* can paralyse decision-making abilities, hindering commitment and focused action.

Calm Thought Focus: Using OM Clarity with your attention in the 'Centre of your Forehead' can bring instant clarity. Some people using this Calm Thought comment that they can literally feel their third eye opening up in the centre of their forehead. The third eye is known as a doorway that leads within to realms of stillness and heightened consciousness. It can be very powerful indeed.

MIND CALM GAME

Enlightened Eye – look out from the centre of your skull

The enlightened eye exercise is an absolutely fantastic way to practise becoming more attuned to the awareness that remains alert throughout your day. Instead of having all of your attention outwards on stuff and movement, you move your attention inwards to look out from the centre of your skull.

The enlightened eye is a gate that leads within to inner realms of still space and higher consciousness. When using this technique you can't help but become more conscious of the silent awareness looking outwards. As you become aware you start to experience your own awareness, which, as we've covered before, is still, silent and spacious.

Instructions

- The Enlightened Eye exercise requires you to notice what it is like to look out from the centre of your skull.

- To do this, pretend that your eyes have magically moved backwards and you can look out from further back in your skull. As you do, notice if your mind becomes quieter and you become aware of the silent watcher within.

PEACE WITH MIND PROTOCOL

Get peace with society

With clarity comes awakened understanding, in which you can see the bigger picture of perfection. For this part of the programme, you are going to use the Peace with Mind Protocol to heal your relationship with any issues relating to society, including:

- Politics
- Laws and regulations
- Social norms
- Religion
- War on terror
- Corporations
- News
- Media

At no point do you have to agree or condone what you might observe in society, only look with compassionate eyes. Using the above list as inspiration, consider what you currently perceive to be a problem in society. Now use the Peace with Mind Protocol to get peace with your thoughts and emotions about the specific issue relating to aspects of society that trouble you.

The six-step Peace with Mind Protocol

1. Perceived Problem

State the problem that you want to heal your relationship with today.

2. Reality Check

Be here now by tuning in and noticing that this moment is happening.

3. Mind Made

Temporarily engage the story in your mind about the problem.

4. Resist Persist

Notice the 'special thought' you are resisting and where you feel it in your body.

5. Bring It On

Let the 'special thought' and feeling be present within you with no resistance.

6. Mind Calm Sitting

Play with 'seeing it, not being it' during a Calm Sitting.

For example, you might be well and truly irritated about the media and hold certain opinions that make you angry. When using the protocol, aim to find your most emotionally charged thought about the media that you are resisting, for example, *the media perpetuates problems*. Now notice where you feel the thought in your body. Once highlighted, adopt the 'bring it on' attitude towards the thoughts and emotions. By letting go of your inner resistance you can return to a more peaceful perspective.

Fighting fire with fire does not work. The best way to increase peace in society is to cultivate calm within you. By using the Peace with Mind Protocol on societal issues that frustrate or worry you, you can be an ambassador for peace and bring about change in a consciously compassionate way.

8

WISDOM

DAILY SCHEDULE

MORNING MIND CALM SITTING
OM WISDOM (Top of Head) Calm Thought only
(Recommended duration: 10–15 minutes or longer if you have the time.)

DAYTIME MIND CALM GAME
Noticing Nirvana: Play with the notion that nothing is wrong

DAYTIME PEACE WITH MIND PROTOCOL
Get peace with TIME, including the past and future

EVENING MIND CALM SITTING
Use all 10 Calm Thoughts
(Recommended duration: 10–15 minutes or longer if you have the time.)

CALM THOUGHT

OM Wisdom (Top of Head)

Calm Thought meaning: Wisdom is not learned, but remembered. Wisdom is born within all of us. It has nothing to do with age or education, and everything to do with your ability to listen beyond the mind to the inner knowing that springs forth when given the still silent space to do so.

Calm Thought purpose: You may not possess learned knowledge about quantum physics, for example, but when it comes to your life, you already have the wisdom you need within you to answer any question you may have. Anyone who has spent time around children will know how wise they can be. They haven't picked up limitations, don't rely too heavily on their mind for answers, and are open to being taught by the inner source of wisdom they were connected to from birth. Growing up we can forget to trust the inner voice or it can become drowned out by the noise of the mind that's working so hard to figure everything out. Wisdom works less on logic or reason and more with intuition and truth.

Calm Thought Focus: Using OM Wisdom with your attention on the 'Top of your Head' – where spiritual teachers have said we are connected to 'omniscient wisdom' – can help you to access the wisdom you need from the source of supreme consciousness with which you are one.

MIND CALM GAME

Noticing Nirvana – play with the notion that nothing is wrong

The belief that there is something wrong is a major hidden source of angst. It is the subtle belief that makes people resist what happens and, in the process, cause themselves a huge amount of unnecessary stress. You cannot control everything that happens, but you can heal the belief that makes what happens so stressful. If you ever find that you are in need of a serene moment, use this technique to bring you back into touch with the inner peace that's present.

Instructions

- Imagine that you can reach inside your mind and pull out the belief that something is wrong. That's right, like magic, the belief that there is something wrong with your body, your life or your world could be completely removed from your mind.

- What's left? Seriously, try that experience on for a few moments and notice what it is like.

The results from the many people I've played this game with have been remarkable. In their eyes I see immediate relief, and comments include that it feels 'free', 'a relief', 'peaceful' and 'expansive', to name only a few. What is it like for you to take a moment to pretend that nothing is wrong? By looking at life through a lens in which nothing is wrong, you start to notice the nirvana that is there, all day every day.

PEACE WITH MIND PROTOCOL

Get peace with time

Wisdom resides within you right now. However, if you're too busy thinking about the past and future you won't be able to benefit from it. Use the Peace with Mind Protocol to heal your relationship with time, including:

- Past trauma
- Future worries
- Resisting what is
- Past failures
- Bad decisions
- Past lives

Using the above list as inspiration, consider what you currently perceive to be a problem relating to your past or future. Now use the Peace with Mind Protocol to get peace with the thoughts and emotions that you are having in relation to things that have happened or might happen.

Reliving and pre-living

The negative side effects of reliving past events and pre-living future scenarios in your mind are huge. You can forever miss real life as it's happening and become lost in endless imagined nightmares that cause much distress.

Getting peace with time is easier when you understand that it's not what's happened that makes you feel bad now, but negatively judging what's happened and then resisting those judgemental thoughts. The same is true for your future concerns. Nothing in your future has the power to cause stress or steal your serenity. Pre-lived future possibilities are only ever thoughts in your mind, which in and of themselves have no power over your present-moment peace. In order to get peace with the past and future you must appreciate that you are not getting peace with what's happened in your past or might happen in the future. You are getting peace with your thoughts and emotions in your mind about the past and future. To escape the Time Trap, use the Peace with Mind Protocol.

The six-step Peace with Mind Protocol

1. Perceived Problem

State the problem that you want to heal your relationship with today.

2. Reality Check

Be here now by tuning in and noticing that this moment is happening.

3. Mind Made

Temporarily engage the story in your mind about the problem.

4. Resist Persist

Notice the 'special thought' you are resisting and where you feel it in your body.

5. Bring It On

Let the 'special thought' and feeling be present within you with no resistance.

6. Mind Calm Sitting

Play with 'seeing it, not being it' during a Calm Sitting.

For example, you might have experienced a traumatic event in your past that, when you think about it today, still causes distress. Using the protocol you want to find the thought (or image) relating to the event that remains emotionally intense. When you do, notice where you feel the thought (or image) in your body. Once you've got both elements, turn your attention to rising above the resistance to let them be present within your body and mind. Remember, the event is in the past and today, as you do this exercise, you are solely getting peace with the thoughts and emotions in your mind about the traumatic event. By 'seeing the mind, not being the mind' you will find the context of calm surrounds the old memory that you're working on.

Having used this protocol with memories or future imaginations, you will be able to think about the past and future without it feeling negative or problematic. I appreciate and honour the fact that really challenging things may have happened or could happen in the future. However, if you want mind calm now, then you need to be willing to learn from the past, accessing your inner wisdom that's always present to give yourself the best chance of enjoying the future you want.

9

ONENESS

DAILY SCHEDULE

MORNING MIND CALM SITTING
OM ONENESS (Far and Wide) Calm Thought only
*(Recommended duration: 10–15 minutes or longer if you
have the time.)*

DAYTIME MIND CALM GAME
Resonance Revolution: Rest in the still presence of life

DAYTIME PEACE WITH MIND PROTOCOL
Get peace with aspects of YOURSELF that you don't love

EVENING MIND CALM SITTING
Use all 10 Calm Thoughts
*(Recommended duration: 10–15 minutes or longer if you
have the time.)*

CALM THOUGHT

OM Oneness (Far and Wide)

Calm Thought meaning: Separation is a mind-made illusion that comes from thinking that you are the voice in your head. There has never been a time or will be a time when you are not connected with everything in the universe. To judge or hate another is to judge or hate yourself. The ultimate love affair in life is oneness with the still silent spacious conscious Self.

Calm Thought purpose: The mind creates a sense of a separate self. If there is a 'me' then there is a 'you' and if there is a 'me' and a 'you' then there is the appearance of 'two'. Mind Calm leads to less identification with the mental constructs of 'me' in your mind. As you let go of who you think you are, the one consciousness that connects and lives with all of 'us' is revealed. Experiencing oneness leads to gentleness, compassion, peace and love. You never fear being alone and never need to prove yourself as better, wiser or more special. You see the world with clarity through compassionate eyes – full of love and wisdom.

Calm Thought Focus: By using OM Oneness with your attention 'Far and Wide', you become awe-stuck and fascinated with the bigness and beauty of infinite consciousness. The desire to engage in the 'mini me' in your mind diminishes, allowing for a healthier relationship with your mind and everything in your life.

MIND CALM GAME

Resonance Revolution – rest in the still presence of life

Now it is time for a more advanced and subtle technique. Still silence resides within everything in physical existence. Every tree and animal, and even everyday objects such as the glass you drink from and the place where you live, have a resonance of stillness to them. To become present and attentive enough to notice the silent resonance of life is to begin to see with fresh eyes the underlying nature of reality. And as you do so, it is impossible not to discover the underlying nature of your real Self.

Instructions

*   Take time and attention to look at inanimate objects with the intention of tuning in and noticing the still silence residing within them.

*   Decide what object you wish consciously to explore and look at it. As you do, intend to notice its inherent stillness. It is still and sitting within stillness. Even if it is moving, there is still an exquisite stillness to it, if you are open to seeing.

*   Look without labelling and just be with the object fully. Feel its presence and, as you do, notice your own.

This technique can bring your world to life and help you to fall back in love with the beauty all around.

PEACE WITH MIND PROTOCOL
Get peace with yourself

Use the Peace with Mind Protocol to heal your relationship with thoughts about yourself, including:

- I'm unloveable

- I'm unwanted

- I'm a bad person

- I'm not good enough

- I'm a fraud

- I'm ugly

- I'm isolated

- I'm selfish

Holding on to self-violent thoughts prevents you from allowing the stunning states of being, infused within the Calm Thoughts, to come to the forefront of your conscious living experience. They also limit your ability to love others and stop you from fulfilling your purpose in this lifetime. Using the above list as inspiration, consider what you currently perceive to be a problem relating to yourself. Then use the Peace with Mind Protocol to get peace with the thoughts and emotions that you are having about a specific issue relating to yourself.

The six-step Peace with Mind Protocol

1. Perceived Problem
State the problem that you want to heal your relationship with today.

2. Reality Check

Be here now by tuning in and noticing that this moment is happening.

3. Mind Made

Temporarily engage the story in your mind about the problem.

4. Resist Persist

Notice the 'special thought' you are resisting and where you feel it in your body.

5. Bring It On

Let the 'special thought' and feeling be present within you with no resistance.

6. Mind Calm Sitting

Play with 'seeing it, not being it' during a Calm Sitting.

For example, you might believe that you are unwanted and, thinking this true, end up with a negative emotion in your stomach. By using the protocol and letting the thoughts and emotions that you would usually want to resist be present within your body and mind, you can release the intense energy of the belief.

Having used this protocol, you should be able to think about the negative belief without it feeling true and move on with your life free from the mind-made limitation.

10

PRESENCE

DAILY SCHEDULE

MORNING MIND CALM SITTING
OM PRESENCE (In Entire Body) Calm Thought only
(Recommended duration: 10–15 minutes or longer if you have the time.)

DAYTIME MIND CALM GAME
Air Aware - look at life from the infinite-eye

DAYTIME PEACE WITH MIND PROTOCOL
Get peace with other aspects of LIFE in general

EVENING MIND CALM SITTING
Use all 10 Calm Thoughts
(Recommended duration: 10–15 minutes or longer if you have the time.)

CALM THOUGHT

OM Presence (In Entire Body)

Calm Thought Meaning: Be still and know who you are. More especially, what you are. You are not your thoughts, emotions, body or life circumstances. You are the conscious awareness that is aware of all these things happening within it. Beyond mind-based ideas about who you are, is the 'peace and love-filled' presence of you.

Calm Thought Purpose: OM Presence helps to bring your attention to the exquisite presence of still, silent, peace-filled big love – which is how it is to experience conscious awareness directly. Become really interested in exploring and enjoying the divine and delicious presence within you, so that your desire to give your mind all of your attention naturally diminishes. Attention wants to go somewhere. Without discovering this presence of consciousness, your attention will end up going on your mind and external life circumstances. You will end up lost in thinking and both peace of mind and peace with mind will elude you. By living attentive to the inner presence of your being, you live in peace, free from mind-made problems.

Calm Thought Focus: Using OM Presence with your attention 'In the Entire Body' brings your attention back into your body after using the OM Universe Calm Thought, which, for some people, may have expanded their attention to the far ends of the universe. This is a great calm thought to end any Calm Sitting, and can help you to engage your day with a greater awareness and appreciation of the perfect peace-filled presence of your being.

MIND CALM GAME

Air Aware – look at life from the infinite-eye

Air Aware is a brilliant game for cultivating mind calm. It may seem like an obvious question to ask, but how many eyes would you say you are looking out of? It goes without saying that you see two eyes when you look in a mirror and other people see two eyes when they look at you. But more intriguingly, how many do you see out of from your own point of view? The response I usually get from the many budding consciousness explorers I've asked is, 'I am looking out from one eye.' Take a moment to notice this for yourself. Although you have two eyes, you are looking out from one eye. In other words, you are looking out from a frameless window of awareness. Some spiritual teachers refer to this as the eye of God but I call it the 'Infinite I'.

Instructions

- To be air aware is to pretend that you have nothing above your shoulders except for one big eye.

- Play with what it's like to look out at the world from one eye, floating in still silent space. Doing so helps to quieten the mind and reconnect you with your real self, which is unbounded conscious awareness.

PEACE WITH MIND PROTOCOL

Get peace with your life

Use the Peace with Mind Protocol to heal your relationship with any other aspects of your life that remain problematic, including:

- Physical condition(s)

- Fear of success

- Negative emotions

- Relationship conflicts

- Career challenges

- Time constraints

- Spirituality

- Modern-day living

Using the above list as your inspiration, consider any other aspects of your life that are currently causing conflict within your mind, you tend to judge harshly and want to reject. Now use the Peace with Mind Protocol to get peace with the thoughts and emotions that you are having about a specific issue relating to your life in general.

The six-step Peace with Mind Protocol

1. Perceived Problem

State the problem that you want to heal your relationship with today.

2. Reality Check

Be here now by tuning in and noticing that this moment is happening.

3. Mind Made

Temporarily engage the story in your mind about the problem.

4. Resist Persist

Notice the 'special thought' you are resisting and where you feel it in your body.

5. Bring It On

Let the 'special thought' and feeling be present within you with no resistance.

6. Mind Calm Sitting

Play with 'seeing it, not being it' during a Calm Sitting.

Having done this protocol, you should be able to think about the life issue without it feeling negative.

Congratulations for completing the programme!

In Closing

THE SPLENDOUR OF SURRENDER

Surrender sits at the heart of Mind Calm. I'm not referring to waving a white flag or giving up, but instead the ability to let go. For you to benefit from everything shared in this book, you must be willing to let go. It is only in being willing to surrender any fixed preconceived ideas about how your mind, body and life should be, that you can fully embrace the joy and grace continuously flowing through every moment of existence.

Let the loving hand of the universe guide you.

GO WITH THE FLOW

Creation is occurring in its awe-inspiring glory right now. To resist life is to push away magic and miracles. Everything happens to help you to wake up, learn how to love unconditionally and live your purpose. Trying to make life look how you think it should is the equivalent of trying to squeeze the universe through the eye of a needle. The universe in which we play is abundant. It is trying to give you everything. Always. There isn't a moment when what you need isn't given to you freely. Yet, if you continue to hold on to the self-imposed limitations in your mind, you can only get, at best, your beliefs about what you think is possible.

Remain open to brand new things showing up. For you to get to where you need to be you must be willing to let your life take you to places that you might think you don't want to go. Go with the flow by living with an accepting heart surrendered to whatever the moment brings. Be willing to receive a helping hand from the universe in ways that you least expect. Be open and expectant of unforeseen miracles.

WALK YOUR TALK

Be a bright light in the lives of the people who cross your path, so that they, too, can see living a peaceful loving life is possible. Everyone is waking up in their unique and special way, and at their own pace. Don't rush the process. Savour it. You are here to get to know your real Self and wake up to what exists beyond the confines of the mind.

Live the teachings and internalize the techniques.

Care less about gathering more concepts and ideas about life and focus your attention on being consciously aware. Without learning how to be in the here and now, no new ideas will be useful because you will remain one step removed from life. Such an attitude of active calmness moves you from possessing knowledge to living with wisdom.

For the most wonderful life, you don't need to 'do anything' inside yourself except be fully attentive to whatever is presented to you each moment. Within you always is supreme consciousness, full of light, love and enlightenment. It's yours for the experiencing. All that's required to inherit its riches is your attentiveness. The more you let go, the more you will find the fullness of still silent space and the perfection of life's unfolding.

SIMPLIFY YOUR LIFE

Fun and fulfilment are impossible if you continue to drive yourself so hard that you cannot enjoy what you have. The endless pursuit of possessions and prestige needs to end, leaving in its place a simplified and humble life.

> *The less you are possessed by possessions, the more mind calm you will personally possess.*

So much time is taken up managing a complicated life that you can end up chasing your own tail. Complexity can end up burning out your body, busying your mind and suppressing your spirit. Although this book is mainly about your inner relationship with life, doing things to make your external life calmer is also hugely beneficial. In essence, if you want mind calm on the inside it helps to simplify your life on the outside. Seven simple ways to bring more calm into your day are:

1. Buy less stuff.

2. Clear the clutter.

3. Downsize where possible.

4. Switch off the TV, phone, computer, tablet and all other electronic distractions for at least one hour every day.

5. Eat real food that is free from man-made extras.

6. Drink more water and fewer stimulants and alcohol.

7. Do absolutely nothing for a few minutes every day.

These simple strategies for simplifying your life add up to a calmer mind and body, and leave space for your spirit to soar. Taking time to do absolutely nothing for even a couple of minutes a day can be profound. Buying less stuff to fill the space and switching off technology every so often can also work wonders, while taking time to savour whomever you are with or whatever you are doing can be the key to connecting to the abundance that life has to offer. In short, it pays dividends to delete the unnecessary complexities and stimulations from your schedule. They all require time, attention and managing. Remember, it's the quality, not quantity, that counts.

There's no place like OM. Make
your home a place of peace.

SURRENDER TO WHAT IS

Without letting this moment be, as it is, then your mind will continue to be busy. Any resistance to life causes the mind to become highly active and remain at the forefront of your attention. You need to make being calm more important than being right and make peace more important than things going to plan. If something unexpected or 'bad' happens, then deal with it gracefully and without any rejection of reality. Wishing things hadn't happened only attaches you to a past that cannot be changed, while pushing back at life only tires you out and puts your peace and prosperity on hold.

$$Resistance = Stress + Struggle$$

$$Surrender = Serenity + Success$$

Resisting reality doesn't change reality; it only makes you stressed and causes unnecessary suffering. Why reject life? Isn't it more appealing to surrender to what is, let things be, as they are, and with a calm mind and courageous heart, take whatever action is required? You can resist what is or you can let the universe give you what you need to wake up to ever-increasing levels of inner peace, joy, love and freedom. This is your choice from now on. Surrender is by far the best strategy if serenity and success is what you genuinely want. Allowing reality to show up in all its glorious and unexpected ways is so much more fun. You have front-row seats at this phenomenal event called your life. Surrender to what is and I guarantee that you will enjoy the boundless benefits of Mind Calm and see with your own awakened eyes that the secret to success is stillness.

Appendix

OVERVIEW OF THE MIND CALM PROGRAMME

This programme can be completed over the duration of 10 days or 10 weeks, depending on your preference. The longer you do it and the more you meditate, the better the results.

1. Connection

Morning Mind Calm Sitting: OM CONNECTION (Soles of Feet) Calm Thought (10–15 minutes, or longer if you have more time).

Daytime Mind Calm Game: Reality Check – tune in to your senses to notice NOW.

Daytime Peace with Mind Protocol: Get peace with aspects of your BODY that you don't like.

Evening Mind Calm Sitting: Use all 10 Calm Thoughts (10–15 minutes, or longer if you have more time).

2. Power

Morning Mind Calm Sitting: OM POWER (Base of Spine) Calm Thought (10–15 minutes, or longer if you have more time).

Daytime Mind Calm Game: Noticing Now Space – see the context of still silent space.

Daytime Peace with Mind Protocol: Get peace with your POTENTIAL to succeed.

Evening Mind Calm Sitting: Use all 10 Calm Thoughts (10–15 minutes, or longer if you have more time).

3. Joy

Morning Mind Calm Sitting: OM JOY (Navel) Calm Thought (10–15 minutes, or longer if you have more time).

Daytime Mind Calm Game: Inward Gazing – be inwardly attentive towards your heart.

Daytime Peace with Mind Protocol: Get peace with the EMOTIONS that you judge as negative.

Evening Mind Calm Sitting: Use all 10 Calm Thoughts (10–15 minutes, or longer if you have more time).

4. Peace

Morning Mind Calm Sitting: OM PEACE (Solar Plexus) Calm Thought (10–15 minutes, or longer if you have more time).

Daytime Mind Calm Game: Heart Watching – look out at life from your heart.

Daytime Peace with Mind Protocol: Get peace with the ENVIRONMENT where you live and work.

Evening Mind Calm Sitting: Use all 10 Calm Thoughts (10–15 minutes, or longer if you have more time).

5. Love

Morning Mind Calm Sitting: OM LOVE (Heart Centre) Calm Thought (10–15 minutes, or longer if you have more time).

Daytime Mind Calm Game: Loving Pink Light – heal the part of you that is them.

Daytime Peace with Mind Protocol: Get peace with your RELATIONSHIPS.

Evening Mind Calm Sitting: Use all 10 Calm Thoughts (10–15 minutes, or longer if you have more time).

6. Truth

Morning Mind Calm Sitting: OM TRUTH (Throat) Calm Thought (10–15 minutes, or longer if you have more time).

Daytime Mind Calm Game: Silence Speaks – be aware of the silence allowing sound.

Daytime Peace with Mind Protocol: Get peace with your CAREER.

Evening Mind Calm Sitting: Use all 10 Calm Thoughts (10–15 minutes, or longer if you have more time).

7. Clarity

Morning Mind Calm Sitting: OM CLARITY (Forehead Centre) Calm Thought (10–15 minutes, or longer if you have more time).

Daytime Mind Calm Game: Enlightened Eye – look out from the centre of your skull.

Daytime Peace with Mind Protocol: Get peace with aspects of SOCIETY that trouble you.

Evening Mind Calm Sitting: Use all 10 Calm Thoughts (10–15 minutes, or longer if you have more time).

8. Wisdom

Morning Mind Calm Sitting: OM WISDOM (Top of Head) Calm Thought (10–15 minutes, or longer if you have more time).

Daytime Mind Calm Game: Noticing Nirvana – play with the notion that nothing is wrong.

Daytime Peace with Mind Protocol: Get peace with TIME including the past and future.

Evening Mind Calm Sitting: Use all 10 Calm Thoughts (10–15 minutes, or longer if you have more time).

9. Oneness

Morning Mind Calm Sitting: OM ONENESS (Far and Wide) Calm Thought (10–15 minutes, or longer if you have more time).

Daytime Mind Calm Game: Resonance Revolution – rest in the still presence of life.

Daytime Peace with Mind Protocol: Get peace with aspects of YOURSELF that you don't love.

Evening Mind Calm Sitting: Use all 10 Calm Thoughts (10–15 minutes, or longer if you have more time).

10. Presence

Morning Mind Calm Sitting: OM PRESENCE (In Entire Body) Calm Thought (10–15 minutes, or longer if you have more time).

Daytime Mind Calm Game: Air Aware – look at life from the infinite-eye.

Daytime Peace with Mind Protocol: Get peace with other aspects of LIFE in general.

Evening Mind Calm Sitting: Use all 10 Calm Thoughts (10–15 minutes, or longer if you have more time).

Be Still.

MAKING MIND CALM YOUR WAY OF LIFE

Academy

Make a positive difference to others by training with Sandy C. Newbigging's award-winning Academy to become a qualified Mind Detox Practitioner (MDM) and/or Mind Calm Meditation (MCM) Coach. For more information, visit www.minddetoxacademy.com

Clinics

Experience a private one-to-one Mind Detox or Mind Calm consultation with Sandy at his UK clinic, or via Skype, or find a Practitioner near you using Sandy's online Practitioner Finder resource.

Courses

Attend a live Mind Calm Meditation class with Sandy and/ or learn even more advanced forms of meditation that are only ever taught in person.

Retreats

Experience Sandy's unique mind–body–soul approach to health, peace and happiness at one of his residential retreats. Highly recommended! For more information, visit www.mindbodyco.co.uk

Online club

Join Sandy's online club where you can access videos, audios, articles and special offers.

For more info, visit: www.sandynewbigging.com

PRESENT THIS BOOK TO GET THESE GIFTS

Having purchased and read this Mind Calm book, you are now entitled to receive the following special offers:

£10 off a Mind Calm Meditation Class

Receive guidance from Sandy C. Newbigging or a qualified Mind Calm Coach. Attending a Mind Calm Meditation class helps you to get the best from Mind Calm. During the class you will learn more about the principles at the heart of this meditation method, gain further support on how to use Mind Calm in your life and also have opportunities to meditate for short periods of time with a group of people – highly recommended!

£50 off a Mind Calm Coach Training Course

Train and qualify as a Mind Calm Coach to share this wonderful way of meditating with others. This course includes a combination of online study and live face-to-face training.

Having graduated you will be able to offer introductory talks; Mind Calm Meditation classes, one-to-one Mind Calm Coaching and host Calm Gatherings. Train personally with Sandy C. Newbigging or with your local Mind Calm Coach Trainer.

Free Mind Calm Gathering

Momentum is vitally important when adopting a new meditation practice. Once you have attended a Mind Calm Meditation class or received Mind Calm Coaching with Sandy, or a qualified Mind Calm Coach, you will then be ready and able to attend a local Mind Calm Gathering. During these short meetings, lasting up to 1.5 hours, you will receive ongoing support from a Mind Calm Coach, have your questions answered and meditate in a group setting – which can be very enjoyable and enhance your experience massively.

Visit www.mindcalm.com for further details.

ABOUT THE AUTHOR

Author photo: Gavin Smith

Sandy C. Newbigging is the creator of the Mind Detox Method and Mind Calm Meditation, and co-creator of the Reawakening Protocol. He has written several books, including *Heal the Hidden Cause, Life Detox, New Beginnings* and *Thunk!* His work has been aired on a number of TV channels including *Discovery Health*. Sandy has clinics in the UK and is available for consultations internationally via Skype; he also runs mind–body–soul residential retreats, and trains Mind Detox, Mind Calm and Reawakening Protocol Practitioner training courses via his award-winning Academy. He was recently commended by the Federation of Holistic Therapists as Tutor of the Year, and has been described by *Yoga* magazine as 'one of the best meditation teachers around'. For more information on talks and workshops given by Sandy C. Newbigging or to book him for a speaking event, please use the following contact details:

answers@sandynewbigging.com

minddetoxman

sandynewbigging

sandynewbigging.tumblr.com

www.sandynewbigging.com